W9-CHY-734

HOPE IS A DIALOGUE

Anthony T. Padovano

© *Copyright 1998 by Anthony T. Padovano*

All rights reserved.

No part of this book may be reproduced in any form,

by photostat, microfilm, xerography, or any other means,

or incorporated into any information retrieval system,

electronic or mechanical, without the written permission

of *CARITAS COMMUNICATIONS.*

All inquiries should be addressed to:

CARITAS COMMUNICATIONS

5526 West Elmhurst Drive

Mequon, WI 53092-2010

414.242.5049...VOICE

414.242.7480...FAX

DGAWLIK@CONCENTRIC.NET...EMAIL

For Theresa

We were married in 1974,
the year *CORPUS* was established

Twenty-five years later I celebrate the
priesthood and marriage her love made
possible.

And I pay tribute to a woman who taught
me that God and Christ are found in the
hope we share with one another.

VI

Cover Art Work

Rosemarie Padovano

VIII

PREFACE

Life stories can be told in different ways. Spiritual journeys may take diverse roads.

The convergence comes about in the end result. If a life story is good, it witnesses to life and gives life. If the spiritual journey is noble, it frees the human heart and honors it.

These essays are at the center of my life story. They are milestones on my spiritual journey.

I offer them in homage to *CORPUS* and the married priests of my own country and the world.

These articles were written from the substance of my life. I offer them to the reader as a gift in the hope that the gift is appropriate, and, whether it is or not, that we can converse and dialogue about hope.

This book is a testimony of hope in the church, the reader, and my own life and, of course, in the God who makes them all possible.

CONTENTS

XII

SETTING STANDARDS

A Paradigm Shift of the Spirit

J esus has become an embarrassment for many church leaders and even for some theologians. The teaching of Jesus is appealed to as a rhetorical standard, but the most credible standard for many in leadership today is "What does the pope wish?" "What did former popes say?" "What is written in the law?" and "What are the political realities of my taking a stand one way or the other?" None of this is wrong in itself, intrinsically evil, *intrinsice malum*, so to speak, but none of it is central.

Reform in the church cannot go very far unless it focuses on what Jesus said clearly. A reform which incorporates these values and gives them priority in ministry and church is the only authentic reform. This reform, I think, requires that we give witness to our faith, rather than merely deal with the politics of reform. The politics is not unworthy. Nonetheless, the deepest hunger in this community is spirituality and a longing for a church more closely aligned with Jesus. In this light, it might be helpful to focus on the parables of Jesus as the foundation for a new ecclesiology.

1

Two major church reformers come immediately to mind, both of them calling us back to the standards that Jesus set. One is Francis of Assisi. He hears a compelling voice cry out: "Francis, my church is in ruins." That line is uttered when the structured church is institutionally very powerful. Under Innocent III, the Roman Catholic Church reached the height of its power, and controlled, for all practical purposes, the entire known world. "Francis, my church is in ruins, because there is structure but so little spirit. Help me rebuild it."

Another great reformer, Martin Luther, observes in the sixteenth century: "If the structure of the church and the pope can do so much, then we do not need Jesus Christ any more." Karl Barth said it another way in the time before the Second Vatican Council when the Roman Catholic Church was powerfully in control, not of the world, but of its own internal life: "I hear the voice of Peter in that church, but where is the voice of Christ? Why does Peter have more to say than Christ? Is this how Peter would have wanted it to have gone?"

Jesus Christ has become an embarrassment for us. When a theologian cites the standard of Jesus, he or she is frequently dismissed as naive, as simplistic, as not sophisticated.

I will divide this reflection into three sections. First I will talk about the parables as a basis for ministry to community. In the second part I will deal with ministry to the marginalized innocent. And, thirdly, ministry to the marginalized guilty. I want to stay with the words of Jesus throughout.

MINISTRY TO COMMUNITY

There was once a man who had two sons. We all know the story. There are no coordinates in the landscape; the parable is psychological; it does not matter where it happened; because it happens everywhere. Its cosmology is human. The man had two sons; they are not named; they are both teenagers; they are less than twenty. They had to be that young because under Jewish custom at the time of Jesus one had to be married by the age of 20 or else one could be brought to the court. They are siblings, of course. There are many sibling stories in Scripture: Cain and Abel, Esau and Jacob, James and John, Martha and Mary, the prodigal son and his brother.

The younger of the two brothers says to his father: "Give me my share of the estate. You are taking too long to die." So the man divided his property between them. It took the younger son a few days to gather all he had. The scene is dramatic. "So you are going", the father must have said. And the son, with embarrassed guilt and rebellious assertiveness, continues the task of gathering, while the father watches confused, ashamed, and filled with heartache. It is a cruel moment in that family's history. "My son will you go away, will you walk with me no more?"

The younger son does what many of us may do at moments in our lives, becoming prodigal and wasteful. He is a young man and all of a sudden he has a fortune. He travels to a distant country, and there he squanders his inheritance in dissolute living. When he had spent everything, a severe famine afflicted the country. Friendships fail when one loses power and money, and so the young man learns a bitter lesson. He is desperate for money for the first time, and hires himself to someone who sends him to feed pigs. At this point the young man has lost even his self esteem. He grew up learning, as all Jews did, "cursed is the one who raises swine".

Jesus brilliantly depicts the scene of anguish and loss, perhaps because he observed it often in the lives of his contemporaries. The young man envies the swine their food. He feels hunger; he has no home and no friends, no family and no money, no self esteem, not even survival skills, (because he was raised in a wealthy family), and he knows that all is his fault.

The contrast is astonishing. A moment before, he has money and is somebody. Then shortly after that he is fighting pigs for food and is aware that he is nobody, that no one cares for him or about him. In a few sentences, Jesus gives us a portrait of unbearable despair.

3

It is only in his wounds that the young man realizes for the first time the damage he has done to his father. The wounds of our lives are sometimes the first claim we have on compassion. But they may also be the first intimation of how we have wounded others. A theme that will occur in the citations that I give is Jesus' insistence that compassion is the hallmark for ministry.

Salvation begins for the young man with his memories. When he is totally depleted, he remembers: "How many of my father's hired hands have bread enough to spare and I am dying of hunger. I will go back and I will say, Father, I have sinned. I know I was foolish, wasteful, destructive. Is there a chance you would let me come home, not as your son (I lost that) but as a slave or a worker.?"

How often we have trained people in the church never to take others back. We leave the divorced and remarried without Communion until they die. Church administrators announce that they will never reconcile married priests and they declare this with pride. Some delight in the exclusion of homosexuals, dissidents, advocates of reproductive freedom. This parable rises up and accuses every one who does not take people back, every one who seeks vengeance when forgiveness alone will heal, every one who asks that justice be done when only mercy will do. The most important thing a parent gives a child, or a church can give its people, is the healing memory it leaves with them.

Memory now breaks through, and the son says: "I shall never be an orphan. All my life I will be part of my father's life. He would no more dismiss me than one member of my body would dismiss another member. My eye can never say to my hand, 'I have no need of you.' And so he will take me back. How do I know that? I know that because I know him, because he has left me with a memory of love. I know that he will not turn me away."

It must have been a thought such as this which brought Peter back to Christ, confessing: "Master, I have failed. I have broken your heart. Could I walk with you again, not close as we once were, that may no longer be possible, but at least on the margin,

4

not at the center where I once was, but at least at the edges?" And Jesus says, "Peter, I love you. Do you love me?" "O Lord, you know that I love you."

So often in the church we do not hear the love because we have discounted the pain. We keep some people at a distance so great that we no longer see their faces or take note of the sound of their voices, their agony, their love.

When we speak as we speak now, there are those in the church who say, "But we must keep our standards. We cannot have reckless and naive forays into love and compassion." We need to answer: "But this is the standard we were given. We must insist less on what we need the other to do for us and more on what the other needs from us." This is ministry. This is truly ministry in the mind of Jesus. "I know my father will never turn against me," the prodigal son says. "He knows my heart is not bad even if my actions have been hurtful."

What memories does the church leave with us? Who in the church are we absolutely certain we could turn to when we are in need? That person is the church for us. That person is the vicar of Christ for our life. Whom would you turn to if everything were wounded in your life? If you had one person to seek out, would you seek out the pope, or the bishop, or the priest? Whom would you seek when you were unsteady, shaky, searching. ? Answer. And in your answer, you will truly know who the church is for you, and where Christ is to be found. Our most lasting ministry is the memories we leave with people. We know that we have failed in ministry when we hear someone say: "I didn't come back because I wasn't sure you would forgive me. I was not certain you would take me back. I was afraid you would hurt me more." When we feel unworthy on every level of life, to whom would we turn? There is the church. The voice and the face of such a person is the voice of the good shepherd and the face of Christ.

And so the young man says: "I will say, Father, be a father to me now when I need a father as I have never before needed a father. O father, I have sinned against heaven and I have hurt you.

5

Don't make me an orphan by saying there is no place in your home or your heart for me. I have no right ever again to be at your table but find at least a crumb for me from the bread of life we once shared. I am not worthy. I have no claim on justice and yet, I ask you, take me back, give me a job, make me a slave, but bring me home." The young man asks that the father not forsake him. Not long after delivering this parable, the storyteller himself will pray a similar prayer from the cross.

Our church must not be a democracy. It must be more than that. It must be a community, In a community, such stories as this parable are possible and believable. But some church administrators object: "Such parables are naive and preposterous. They were for an earlier moment in the church, but they work no more." How far we have come! This parable measures the distance. How wrong a road we have taken in our prodigal search for orthodoxy and the right direction! Many in our church have bartered our inheritance as a community for a bowl of porridge. We give up our identity as a community and home and become an institution and no more than that, a church in ruins, when we make this parable rhetoric rather than policy. We cannot close our ears to all the lost sons and daughters in our midst without becoming also deaf to Christ.

The story goes on. While the young man was still far off, the father saw him. I wish we could capture this moment on film: the face of the father, his eyes, the body language. It was a long wait. It took time for the young man to squander that much money. The father waited. "Will I die before I see my son again? How did I fail him as a father? Why did money mean more to him than my love?" The father had looked often down the road that took his son away. "My son was once there, why can't he be there again? Come back, my son, not only so that I can heal you, but so that you can forgive me for not having been more." And then Jesus says, "When he saw him," and this is the crucial line, "he was filled with compassion." The hallmark of ministry. The father does not yet know if the son has returned for forgiveness. He might be returning only for more money. No matter. The sight of the son is

6

gift for the father. Sometimes, the presence of someone is all we want and more than we need.

The young man is frightened. It is the first time he has come near home and been frightened of his own home. Is this how some Catholics feel as they enter our churches? The son is determined. Love is a paradox of daring and diffidence. And so he continues. Then Jesus says, "The father ran to him." The entire gospel and the entire church can be summed up in that line. The father ran to him. The son seeing the father running to him knows that he is truly home. There are no words spoken. The father puts his arms around his son and kisses him as the son falls into his father's arms like a shipwrecked mariner.

Then the speech which all of a sudden is not as necessary or as difficult to deliver as it once seemed to be: "Father, I have hurt you. I am not worthy to be called your son. Don't hurt me, don't hate me, don't turn me away. If you will not give me life or take me in, where can I go?" The young man speaks the language of defeat, the language we all speak when our resources are depleted. All that the father hears is the first word: Father. No other word matters. The father answers with a liturgy. He vests his son with symbols of celebration and acceptance. "You are not a slave. This is my son", he says to the servant. "Bring him not the work clothes of a slave, but the best robe we have, not the yoke of submission, but a ring on his finger, not bare feet but sandals," A son, never a slave, wears robes and rings and sandals.

The liturgy of the word, so to speak, ends here as syllables and symbols and vestments bring us to the breaking of the bread.

The father moves from compassion to communion, ready to offer the bread of life, not the crumbs of sterility. Jesus once asked what kind of a father would give a son a stone when he came for bread? The communion table, you see, is for those who need it most. What could possibly have led us to put in our missalettes and in our law that non-Catholics must not approach our table to receive communion? Could we have made such rules in a church built on parables?

7

We know of course the story of the elder son. He is angry. He is bitter. He is part of the communion police. Law over sacrament. Filled with anger, he is a harsh official, rather than a son of the same father. He makes a brilliant case for vengeance. It is often easier to make a case for vengeance than for forgiveness. Contrast the way each brother addresses the father. "Look, you", the angry son cries. The younger son had said, "Father." Then the elder son tells us where he really is, where so many in the church still are: "I have slaved for you all my life." The younger son had pleaded, "Take me home." "I never disobeyed your orders," the older son continues. Note the words, "your orders." The older son has built a life on obedience, feeling uncomfortable with love and forgiveness.

The self–righteous lawgiver makes obedience the highest norm. What happens to a church when allegiance to the pope's orders is the basic reason for ministry? "I never disobeyed your orders." Ironically, it is the older son who is the slave in that home, not because the father wishes it but because the older son perceives life this way. The elder son shouts out in anger, "but this son of *yours*" He says in effect what so many Catholics unfortunately can say: "I don't want to be part of a family that forgives. If there is amnesty for married priests and for the divorced and remarried, I don't want to be part of that family. I would rather be bitter like the elder brother, and I wish to be that because I hate my life and I hate everything that I have been forced to do in it." Such a small church! Such piteously diminished spirits! Hearts of stone!

The real prodigal is the elder son who has wasted his entire life. All that the younger son wasted was money. The elder son attacks the father, never using the term "father".

There is always a peril in forgiving. We may become the victim of the anger of those whose lives are filled with rage and resentment.

The elder son's smallness contrasts with the father's generosity. "My son", he says, "all I have is yours." The father had come out of the house to plead with the elder son. Going out to the son is against Jewish custom; yet the father does this for both sons. The father makes a desperate effort to bring his first son to love. "Your brother was lost. I can't afford to lose him again."

The parable reminds us that we cannot hold a family or a community together with justice. Justice is for strangers and institutions. Justice is what a community settles for when it has lost its heart. Love finds justice deficient and confining. Love prepares a feast while justice counts the calories.

Let me end this first section with one other image of ministry from the Gospels. Jesus got up from the table, took off his outer robe, tied a towel around himself, poured water into a basin, and began to wash his disciples' feet and to wipe them with the towel that was tied around him. John, of course, as we are well aware, is the only evangelist who does not give us the breaking of the bread at the Last Supper. The sacrament of the Last Supper for him is service and ministry raised to the highest standard in the washing of the feet. The disciples were astonished because Jesus at this moment takes on the social role of a woman and a slave. Only women and slaves washed people's feet.

Jesus comes to Simon Peter: "Lord, are you going to wash my feet?" Jesus observes, "You don't know what I am doing, but later you will understand." Peter counters, "You will never wash my feet, never, never; you will never wash my feet." Then Jesus said, "Peter, if I do not wash your feet, you cannot be part of me." And Peter said, "Lord, my hands and my head as well." A powerful moment between Peter and Christ. After he washed their feet, he put his robe on, returned to the table and said, "Do you know what I have just done for you? You call me Teacher and Lord, and that is what I am. If I, the Lord, have washed your feet, you must do this for one another."

In Matthew, Jesus observed: "If your son asks for bread, do you give him a stone? If your daughter asks for a fish, do you give her a snake? You know how the irreligious lord it over others and how their leaders are always conscious of who has authority and who does not. It must never be that way with you. Never!"

Jesus then continues, "I will not leave you orphans. This is my commandment, that you love one another as I have just loved you."

It is so simple. How did we miss it? "I do not call you slaves or servants."

The parable of the prodigal son is the echo of all this teaching. "I have called you friends. You are my friends."

What kind of a man would think of the parable we have just heard or would do what he did in the washing of the feet. ? What would have entered into his mind to do such things? What a magnificent heart he had! What kind of a church should have come from this? How did we get it wrong? Why did we get it wrong? Why don't we make it right now?

MINISTRY TO THE MARGINALIZED INNOCENT

The second level of ministry that emerges from the parables is ministry to the marginalized innocent. What I would like to consider in this regard is the parable of the Good Samaritan. Jesus again contrasts law with compassion

A lawyer stood up to test him, "Teacher, what must I do to inherit eternal life?" Jesus says, "What's in the law?" And the lawyer says, "You will love the Lord, your God, with all your heart and soul and strength and mind, and your neighbor as yourself." Then Jesus, moving him from orthodoxy to orthopractice, says, "You've given the right answer. Do this and you will live." The lawyer is embarrassed because the answer is too simple. He wants something more complicated: "Who is my neighbor?" Jesus then tells the story of the Good Samaritan. To give it context, there are some things we should know.

It is 23 miles from Jerusalem to Jericho, a long, and perilous journey. Jerusalem is 2,250 feet above sea level, Jericho is 900 feet below sea level, For this reason, one goes "down" to Jericho even though Jericho is north of Jerusalem. Wealthy people live in

Jericho, most of the priests, unfortunately. The road, therefore, was filled with robbers and was dangerous. Travel in the ancient world was always risky,

A man fell into the hands of robbers. They stripped him, they beat him and they left him to die. The first person who comes down the road after the assault is a priest. He sees the man and passes to the other side of the road; partly because victims are an inconvenience, partly because legal impurity could happen if a priest touches a bleeding body. In the action of the priest we see the God whom that priest worshiped was a God of laws rather than a God of life. There is always a good reason to pass by, especially in the ancient world when one never traveled for frivolous reasons.

Then a levite passed by. A levite would be a temple official, clergy. He too passes on the other side.

One might imagine the lawyer was becoming uncomfortable at this point. Many of his connections in Jerusalem were with priests and levites and they are not being presented favorably in this parable. Then a Samaritan comes by with good reasons to ignore the dying man: *religious reasons* -this man who is dying is a heretic; *social* reasons - a Samaritan does not deal with a Jew; *historical reasons* - Samaratans and Jews have plundered each other's lives and homes; *psychological reasons* - the Samaritan is traveling on urgent business; and *personal reasons* - it is a messy situation and one that may not be appreciated by the person one assists.

Jesus is disturbing his audience by making a Samaritan the hero of the story.

The Samaritan approaches the dying man. He is filled with compassion. One traveled in the ancient world with a first aid kit consisting of wine and oil: wine, an antiseptic and oil, a curative. The Samaritan responds very concretely to the victim: wine and oil, then bandages. He picks the man up, holds him in his arms, puts him on a donkey, and brings him to an inn. This time there is room in an inn. The God of Israel, in effect, Jesus is saying, is a

God of mercy. The Samaritan takes out two denarii, about a hundred dollars, and also leaves an open account. "Take care of him and when I come back I'll pay all the costs."

As the story ends, Jesus turns the table and asks the lawyer, "Which of the three is the neighbor? Which one is the minister: the priest, the temple official, or the one we have been taught to despise? Which of the three is the neighbor?" How different questions sound when we make them concrete! Let us try concrete questions in terms of problems in today's church. Why can't my father celebrate liturgy publicly anymore? Because he had me as a son? Why can't my sister celebrate liturgy? Because she is a woman. But she loves God and people. Is my homosexual brother intrinsically evil in his actions? Then why don't I feel the evil around him? Why is it when I'm near him I can only sense the fact that he loves? Is my mother less a woman because she found love only in her second marriage?

We make such cruel distinctions in the church, especially when we make the legal standard more demanding than the existential situation. Do we not often say to priests: In pastoral life and in secret you may always be compassionate, but be compassionate only selectively in public? Compassion ruins your career and you will embarrass the church. If you must be compassionate controversially, do it behind closed doors in the internal forum, in the confessional, on a deathbed.

Jesus forgave recklessly, openly. Should not this be our standard?

The lawyer who chooses not to say the word Samaritan, he hates it so much, finally gives the right answer, "The one who had compassion, the one who had pity in his heart." Jesus says, "You've got it. That's right."

When that young Jewish man beaten on the open road woke up a few days later he must have been changed forever. "Who brought me here? How did I get here?" As he heard the story, he must have been profoundly moved. He could never, after this, teach his children, as he was once taught, to hate Samaritans. And so the healing is spiritual as well. Why is it we do not take greater risks for compassion? What makes us use the name of Jesus to justify what Jesus would never, could never do?

MINISTRY TO THE MARGINALIZED GUILTY

The woman has no name. She is known only by her crime or her sin. It is always that way when we are ready to execute people. We refer to them by their crime or their sin. Their name does not matter. She is a woman, which already means she is of little account socially. She is an adulteress and that, of course, does not help.

Notice what Jesus does in these parables and actions: he tells us about a son who did not obey and he rescues him; about a Samaritan who was rejected by the institution and he exalts him. He washes people's feet which is what a free Jewish man was told he must never do. The common thread, in every instance, is compassion over law.

The woman will be used to make a point. Women frequently are used to make a point. She is to be executed for adultery. There is an incredible intersection here between authority, sex and property. The Jewish community linked adultery with property rather than with sex. This is why, under Jewish law, if a single Jewish woman had sex with a married man, it was not adultery because she was not property. But if a single man had sex with a married Jewish woman, it was adultery because she was someone else's property. In any case the death of this woman will be an irrelevance.

The great fear of many people about the church is that if we are compassionate this will create license. Some would look at the prodigal son and say, "If we let the son get away with that, a third of his father's estate, family life will disintegrate." The woman taken in adultery, "If we let women get away with that, marriage will disintegrate." With the Samaritan, "If people know that ministry happens outside our system, especially with those to whom ministry is forbidden, the church will disintegrate." There are large groups of people in our church who seem to be preoccupied with disintegration.

This story is filled with the language of power and law. What it says is that sometimes a woman's death is necessary so that the system can work. If she dies, it's a price worth paying for order in the system. Today we say that order in the church is important, and we are willing to pay a high price in human lives and human happiness in order to keep the system working. If people no longer have the gospel preached or get pastoral care, it is a small price to pay, some suppose, so that the system will work in the way we prefer. At some point, however, the price for order is the loss of order and the whole community is left in disarray. At times the price we pay for order is giving up love and honesty and even the gospel.

I have always been intrigued by the fact that Matthew, Mark and John begin the passion story with a woman performing an anointing. Luke does not, although he is the one who emphasized the role of women in his gospel. We find this story of the woman in adultery in the eighth chapter of John, but scripture scholars agree that the Greek in this passage is Luke's and that it belongs at the end of chapter 21 or the beginning of chapter 22. This is where Luke begins the passion narrative. It is a powerful introduction!

It is early in the morning as this story unfolds. Jesus comes to the temple, the symbol of institutional authority. Jesus is in Jerusalem. People come to him and he begins to teach.

The scribes and pharisees bring in a woman who had just been caught in adultery. Jesus knows their faces. He knows they are hostile. He is in Jerusalem. He is at the temple, and he is soon surrounded by enemies. The accusers make the woman, marked for death, stand before all of them. "Teacher, this woman was caught in the act of committing adultery." The woman is being used, degraded by being forced to stand there, treated as an object.

Jewish law was savage. An adulterous woman must be stoned

to death immediately. That would have happened to Mary had Joseph decided to press charges. Every Jewish woman knew that. This Jewish woman knew that. It was written in Leviticus and Deuteronomy and women were told this from their earliest years. It will not be the last time religious people will suppose that violence may be pleasing to God.

They said all of this, of course, so that they might have a charge to bring against him. So the woman is only a means to an end. Jesus bent down and wrote with his finger on the ground, and then he delivered a haunting line. "If there is someone who has never committed a sin, let that person begin the execution." He continues writing on the ground. Embarrassed, they start to walk away, slowly, in order, reluctantly. Jesus was left alone with the woman standing before him. "Woman, is there no one left to condemn you?" The only time she speaks, "There is- there is no one." "Nor will I condemn you." I don't know if she had seen Jesus before, but even if she had, she sees him differently now, because the face of the deliverer always looks different in the act of deliverance.

CONCLUSION

We have heard stories of a lost son in one parable, of a lost daughter in the woman caught in adultery, of a Samaritan who saved a dying Jew, and of a Teacher who washed the feet of his disciples. The common thread is that ministry is defined by the need others have of us.

What are the needs today? Not more rules, I believe. Just imagine if the rules were followed in the parables and actions of Jesus: the prodigal son would have been sent away, the woman in adultery would have been killed, the Samaritan would have left the man alone to die, and the washing of the feet could not have been done by Jesus because a male who was free could not do this. Don't we see what Jesus is trying to say about ministry and church? Why is it we have eyes to see and do not see? Who gives us the right to withhold healing and to do this in the name of Christ? How can we fit the church into these parables, especially when church policy is identified with the wrong characters in the parables? Church policy is, too often, the elder brother, angry, demanding obedience and vengeance, Church policy is the Jewish priest on the open road rather than the good Samaritan. Does anyone know a Catholic priest who was ever dismissed from ministry for not being compassionate? Church policy is the oppressor of women keeping them in their place, especially punishing them when the offenses are sexual.

I have a tremendous problem and I need to share this with you personally in explaining my own marriage. My church says to me that the only obstacle to my coming back into full canonical ministry is that my wife is alive. The real reason is not a so-called broken promise because I shall be welcomed back if my wife dies even though the promise was still, supposedly, broken. What the church needs from me to be restored to canonical ministry is a death certificate. A live woman is an obstacle to the canonical priesthood, but a dead woman, the mother of my children, a disciple of Christ through and through, a dead woman will lift the obstacle. How did we get from Christ to this?

Jesus is such an embarrassment. What kind of a God could be served by such a law? One of the most beautiful things that has happened to us since Vatican II is that you and I have started to believe, as we never did before, in a church of love rather than a church of law. A church, therefore, that makes more of obedience than compassion, which withholds forgiveness and reconciliation and prefers to punish the prodigal son, which no longer sees the victims of its own policies on the open roads of life and which passes to the other side rather than to minister to their needs, which picks up stones to keep women on the margins, which insists on the law excluding women from the sanctuary, which does not value women for their needs and gifts, such a church has stopped being the church of Christ. A church which silences all its prophets is a church which would crucify Jesus again.

Jesus is an embarrassment for those who favor institution and law. They place their security in those they see: the pope or bishops or pastors. "Blessed are those who have not seen and still believe."

What we have done, unfortunately, in acting against these parables, is to have built temples of exclusion and oppression, introduced the slavery of law and brought back sacrifice, not of animals, but of people's self-worth, believing that God would be glorified in their destruction.

The parables remain outside the temple and there we find Christ. God, after all, sent us Christ, not a church. We shall not find our way again until faith in Christ is more visible than our faith in church.

A true Christian creed should now confess: It was always you, gracious God, whom we sought. You were the mother and the father we longed for and never found, the son we embraced coming back to us after so much longing for his return. It was always you, gracious God, you were the healer who came to us as we were wounded and neglected on the open roads of life. You were the deliverer, the unexpected stranger, who gave us compassion. You were the one who took us in your arms when no one else would, who lifted us up from the dirt and the danger where we were beaten. It was always you. You were the one who poured water in a basin and came and washed our feet. It was always you. Remember us when you enter into paradise. Do not leave us behind at the door as our church can do so easily, not counting the cost or the pain it inflicts. We can only be safe in the church, if we are first safe in you, because it is only you who are infallible, never failing, always renewing. It was always you, was it not? This is the great truth we have learned on our journey of life. We ask you now to bring us home, to put rings on our fingers and sandals on our feet, and hold us. It was always you. Call us your sons and daughters once more and let us call you father and mother once again. Bring us to your table where in the breaking of the bread we will recognize you. Then send us out as ministers of compassion to a world whose heart is broken. Wash our feet so that we shall never forget your commandment of love. When our task is done, bring us home and tell us that we were worthy and let us know we did some good and even show us the faces of those we healed. Then we shall have found the church, for in finding you we find the church and in losing you we lose everything. It was always you, gracious God. You have called us by name, and in hearing our name, we have found, in your voice, a Shepherd, a Savior, and the Church of Christ.

CATHEDRAL TO CONSCIENCE CATHOLICISM

Building the City of God

John Henry Newman offered his famous toast to conscience first and the papacy second in the midst of the turbulence surrounding the definition of papal infallibility. That was well over a century ago.

Newman had it right. Conscience is more than the papacy in Catholic teaching and theology even if not always in Catholic practice.

Over the last century, papal infallibility has devalued the Ecumenical Council so that Catholics often consider the Ecumenical Council not as an event in its own right but as another way in which the pope may choose to govern the Church. Indeed, many bishops view the Council in this manner.

The Ecumenical Council is a structure which presupposes conscientious dissent and theological difference and is not intimidated by it. When final decisions are made in the Council, they incorporate a large range of views and are often, therefore, resilient.

21

Papal infallibility, however, makes it far more likely that consistency of thought on all issues will become the norm for the Church. I am calling this regimentation Cathedral Catholicism, an *ex cathedra* Catholicism of power and orthodoxy.

Papal infallibility, furthermore, oriented Catholic theology to the papacy rather than to the university. University theology in the Middle Ages, patristic theology before that, did not seek papal approval. It was unlikely that theologians would impugn the Catholicism of their opponents or quote the pope to give their theories credibility.

It is noteworthy that when Martin Luther posted the ninety–five theses, he did not expect a Reformation. These were issues, albeit incendiary, which theologians felt proper to debate in public.

One of the casualties of papal infallibility, perhaps the most catastrophic casualty, has been Conscience Catholicism. The Second Vatican Council sought to redress this loss by calling for a collegial Church. It also strengthened Conscience Catholicism by its Declaration on Religious Freedom. It is important to observe that a Council, not a pope, rescued conscience in this instance and reversed the silencing of a theologian, John Courtney Murray, who was the main architect of this teaching.

It is also instructive to recall that the papacy was unwilling to proclaim the primacy of conscience, soon after the Council, when Paul VI refused to allow conscience to be a determining factor in issues of artificial birth control. Indeed, the pope moved against conscience even though the overwhelming majority of the various papal commissions called for a change in the teaching and even after Cardinal Suenens warned of an equivalent Galileo case if there were no change. Moreover, the pope decided against conscience precisely because his predecessors had done so and specifically because, he assumed, that a lack of consistency in papal teaching would undermine papal authority.In the furor, a century ago, over papal infallibility, a number of prominent Catholic theologians suffered penalties and excommunication. John Henry

Newman observed that an eagerness to believe whatever the Church teaches as official policy may be a sign that one has little faith and no conviction and is, therefore, prepared to accept anything at all. The fact that the vast majority of bishops today will endorse whatever a new pope declares on all controversial issues now troubling the Church is one example of the faith Newman criticized.

How profound is one's faith and conviction if one experiences no difficulty in changing course easily once a higher authority orders this? How does one do this with integrity and without shame after one has condemned and punished people for accepting the very positions one is now prepared to proclaim as true? Do we not see in this sad behavior the fruits of Cathedral Catholicism?

GIVING TRUTH A CHANCE

Where Cathedral and Conscience Catholicism meet is in the desire to discover the truth. Cathedral Catholicism, as I understand it, transfers the act of faith into an act of obedience. Conviction is not as important as submission. Cathedral Catholicism assumes that people at large are incapable of the truth and that a small number of Catholics, with the proper juridical authority, are its essential guarantors. Cathedral Catholics believe that the truth is given to this small group, eventually to just one person.

Conscience Catholicism deals with the act of faith in its own terms. It links faith to the community not by obedience but by a desire to belong. Cathedral Catholicism pertains to the community by obedience; Conscience Catholicism, by participation in the life of the community. So–called Cafeteria Catholics care about belonging to the church but refuse to violate their conscience or their integrity to do so. Conscience Catholics assume that people at large always find the truth and that the smaller the number the less likely it is that the truth will be encountered and the more likely it is that the small group will be self–serving. Conscience Catholicism believes that Pentecost was for all believers, not perhaps all playing the same role but all having a meaningful voice.

The Second Vatican Council affirmed in its Declaration on Religious Freedom: "The truth cannot impose itself except by virtue of its own truth; as such, it enters the mind quietly and powerfully."

This is the only way the truth works. Even if we compel someone else to accept a truth we believe in, the other will not receive it as a truth but only as a command. What would religion gain from forcing people to accept a truth they do not believe in, a truth they do not find personally convincing? Is not the point of all religion the captivation of the heart? The heart, however, can never accept a truth the mind rejects.

When I speak of Cafeteria or Conscience Catholicism, I do not mean that one may have contradictory opinions on essential items in the church's faith. Luther, I believe, gave us a helpful norm here. Articles of faith must be validated by Scripture. Scripture is compelling but not coercive. It proclaims the Word as Good News, not by imperatives and edicts with juridical force.

I maintain that there is no crisis of faith anywhere in the church with regard to essential faith issues. Thus, Catholics accept God as a loving Parent and Christ as God's Word and our Redeemer. They believe in the invincible power of the cross and in the Easter life which comes from it. They affirm that God is encountered in a community of believers and that Christ is present in the sacramental life of the Church. One can extend the list. There is no need to do so.

It is an especially perfidious act to drive from the church or to its margins Catholics who accept all these core items, the very substance of faith in Christ, but who do not accept teaching which emerged late in Christian history, often with no biblical validation, and, indeed, frequently imposed by force.

If there is truth in these lesser teachings, believers will discover this for themselves; the larger truths they accept will lead them sooner or later to see the value of these lesser truths if these indeed have value. It is, furthermore, the capacity to live in the church with honor and love which gives one the best chance to perceive all that is true in it and to accept this with internal assent.

Thomas Carlyle, the essayist, once observed: "No lie lives forever." Why is it difficult for many church officers to accept this optimistic reading of human conscience and human life?

Jesus told us that the truth would make us free. But how can we be made free by a truth which is forced upon us so that we live in the prison of its imposition? Did not Paul tell us that it is by freedom we are set free? How is there freedom to encounter and internalize the truth if one is given no choice and if one's conscience is seen as a liability? The appeal to conscience is viewed suspiciously by many church officers. One is made to feel somehow less a Catholic for having a conscience. Even if one receives a hearing before such church officials more often than not it is expected that one will present oneself timidly and even apologetically for having had a conscience and for burdening the Church with its demands.

Is it not difficult to reconcile all this with the gospel? Is it not impossible to imagine Jesus favoring this approach, the same Jesus who dissented from aspects of Judaism in conscience and who embraced the marginalized, the very Jesus who insisted that the marginalized must never be scandalized by the imperious behavior of church officers?

THERE IS NO CHANGE WITHOUT TURMOIL

Jesus does not bring about change with Zen–like serenity. The gospel shows us a Jesus in active engagement and verbal confrontation, under arrest and condemned to death. The New Testament Church follows this pattern. The disciples resist and protest and they, too, endure excommunication, vilification, imprisonment and execution.

If Jesus and the New Testament Church could not achieve their objectives without turmoil, how can we? Reform Catholics are sometimes charged with an impatience born of spiritual immaturity. In some cases, of course, the charges are valid. But in most instances accusers seek by such accusations to silence all prophetic witness.

Nietzche once wrote: "The world does not revolve around those who create great upheavals but around those who create new values."

The new values, as Jesus discovered and the New Testament Church experienced, cannot be brought to birth without struggle and a measure of disorder. Birth is a turbulent and messy business. It is, nonetheless, not something the human family wishes to forego so that order and quiet might be maintained.

Frederick Douglas astutely noted:

"Those who favor freedom and depreciate agitation are men who want crops without planting the ground. They want rain without thunder and lightning. They want the ocean without the roar of the many waters."

It would be difficult to find someone who defended papal prerogatives more ardently than Cardinal Bellarmine did. Newman, in an 1874 letter to the Duke of Norfolk, quotes Bellarmine:

"Bellarmine, speaking of resisting the Pope, says 'In order to resist and defend oneself no authority is required...Therefore as it is lawful to resist the Pope if he assaulted one's person, so it is lawful to resist him if he assaulted souls...It is lawful, I say, to resist him by not doing what he commands and hindering the execution of his will.'"

Here, in the United States, Archbishop Kenrick once wrote of the Pope in a widely used moral theology text:

"His power was given for edification...If he uses it from the love of domination (quod absit) scarcely will he meet with obedient populations."

Dissent by reformers must always be done for the church. Dissent is an act of conscience seeking commitment to the church. It is foolish to expect that dissent will be met with joy and eagerness in all quarters. When it is not, humility and courage are in order. If the dissent is not of God it will perish. If it is of God, the dissent is invincible.

In dissent, then, we raise questions which must be answered if the church we love is not to perish from an incongruity between Church and Christ.

We ask, for example:

▷ Why is sexual misconduct condemned so readily but not violence, warmaking, and the death penalty?

▷ Why are there harsh words for those who speak out prophetically but not for those who suppress free speech?

▷ Why are new ideas punished but not the imposition of dead ones?

▷ Why are resignations from public ministry excoriated but not tenure in office that is harmful?

▷ Why are those who promote women criticized but not those who oppress women?

▷ Why are canonical penalties invoked against those who celebrate the weddings of divorced and remarried Catholics but not against those who vilify such Catholics or, worse, urge women to remain with abusive husbands?

▷ Why is there a termination of canonical ministry for priests who marry but not for priests who divorce themselves from their community's needs and abuse its life?

▷ Why are those who question that the pope is infallible discredited but not those who surrender their conscience to him?

▷ Why are church officers scandalized by those who ignore canon law but not by those who neglect the gospel?

▷ Why are those who sign a referendum for reform censured but not those who administer an annulment and celibacy dispensation process that encourages dishonesty and rewards it?

27

▷ Why is there compassion for conservatives troubled by church reform but none for Catholic reformers disturbed by church rigidity?

▷ Why is there anger at those who indict pastoral leaders for harming the church but nor for those who support insensitive bishops and urge them to persecute liberal Catholics?

▷ Why are those who call for justice in the church deemed troublesome but not those who claim the church is perfectly just in every aspect of its life?

▷ Why are those who seek an inclusive church thought to be a danger but not those who excommunicate and hound Catholics from the church?

▷ Why are church officers so ready to indict secular governments which deny their citizens equality before the law but so unwilling to protest when canon law denies legal equity in the church?

These questions must not be left unanswered if this church is truly to be Christ's church. They must not be left unaddressed if this church is to be a safe church for us and our children, and for the disenfranchised and the marginalized who need the church and yearn to be a meaningful part of it.

THE HEART OF THE MATTER

If what we have said thus far is granted, a problem remains. By citing Conscience or so–called Cafeteria Catholicism as more acceptable than Cathedral Catholicism, do we open the way for people to believe anything they want and then justify it in the name of conscience? Do we open the church, thereby, to such individual and capricious behavior and belief that the church would not become a community of believers?

Let us begin by observing that Cathedral Catholicism does not give us a community of believers as much as an assembly of servile church members. There are, then, problems whichever way we go.

Conscience or so–called Cafeteria Catholicism must be judged not in terms of whether it is perfect but in terms of whether it is close to the gospel and in terms of its fruits and its pastoral ability to bring people to Christ.

We might add, furthermore, that Cathedral Catholicism will not be effective in the contemporary world. When people are given no voice and when their lives and witness count for nothing, people do not truly believe in the way the gospel requires.

Let me take as one example the approach to birth control. Cathedral Catholicism gives credence to only one person in reaching the decision on birth control. This one person is not married and almost all counsultors on the various papal commissions were not. The witness of married Catholics, sensitive, intelligent, committed Catholics, their witness over the years rejecting this teaching in theory and in practice and rejecting it in virtually unanimous numbers makes no difference. Only bishops who are not open on this question are now appointed and they are appointed with the clear intention of prohibiting even conscientious and respectful dissent from this teaching. We know all this.

Cathedral Catholicism insists on compliance, dismisses as valid the experience of married couples on this question and calls for silence and obedience. How does this approach create community and help all God's People to find the truth together?

We need, nonetheless, to speak of the boundaries within which Conscience or so–called Cafeteria Catholicism must function if is to be responsible. Let us review these.

CONSCIENCE CATHOLICISM PARTICIPATES IN THE LIFE OF CATHOLIC COMMUNITY AND DOES NOT ABANDON IT

The community life of the church helps so–called Cafeteria Catholics find truth in community and not only individually. Conscience Catholicism loves the church and trusts it. It is able to do this not only because the quality and character of the people who make up the church are impressive but also because history shows the church as overcoming its limitations time and again. Conscience Catholicism, then, allows the community life of the church to become a boundary within which it operates. This community life becomes the great teacher of Conscience Catholicism. Conscience Catholicism chooses Catholicism because of the way the church lives its life, not because of its teaching only. Indeed Conscience Catholicism is able to find better teaching in other Christian churches on a number of issues. The church, after all, is not an academy where one goes to hear the truth but a community where one comes to live it.

CONSCIENCE CATHOLICISM ACCEPTS A PREFERENTIAL OPTION FOR MAGISTERIUM AND TRADITION

It begins by expecting to find truth in the present and inherited teaching of the official church. It does this readily because the church has so often been right on the essential issues which give our faith solidity: the reliability of the gospel, the identity and definition of who Jesus is, the trustworthy witness and interpretation of the cross and Easter, the meaning of sacramental life and community in the power of God's Spirit.

CONSCIENCE CATHOLICISM IS READY TO HEAR CAREFULLY OTHER THAN MAGISTERIAL VOICES IN THE CHURCH AND IT IS INFLUENCED BY THEM

When magisterial voices seem to have missed the point,

Conscience Catholicism hears, instead, the voices of those in the community who seem able to speak credibly in the name of Christ and with the authority of the Spirit. Conscience Catholicism believes that it is far more likely that the pope may be misled than that the community at large may err.

CONSCIENCE CATHOLICISM MAKES A CLEAR DISTINCTION BETWEEN WHAT IS ESSENTIAL TO FAITH AND WHAT IS MARGINAL

Conscience Catholicism is profoundly committed to the core of the Gospel and the Catholic Tradition. The most effective way to discern this core is to seek in Scripture the themes which are continually repeated in its books and the themes on which the New Testament church staked its life. We have cited some of these themes already. These themes are so constant and solid that they are affirmed by all the Christian churches even when these churches separate from one another. The validity of the marginal issues is judged by their relationship to essential issues and not simply by virtue of their having been officially declared as Catholic doctrine.

These then are some boundaries within which we seek to define Conscience or so–called Cafeteria Catholicism. We do not seek to dissent for personal convenience but to discover what it is to which we say "yes" and to offer our lives to it. Conscience Catholicism seeks the core of belief which is worthy of our faith and love.

QUESTIONS OF CREDIBILITY AND CONSEQUENCES

A new millennium is fast approaching. It is a time when the papacy can play an important role for the church and for the world. The pope has asked in a recent encyclical, *Ut Unum Sint,*, how his ministry might better serve the Christian Community. He asked Christians to give him advice. I am prepared to do that. I suggest that papal teaching in the contemporary world is better done in symbols than in words. Catholics have always been effective with symbols.

31

The church at large rejects much of the teaching of John Paul. Surveys and polls around the world give evidence of this. So does the exodus of laity from parishes and clergy from canonical ministry and women religious from vowed community life.

The church does not, however, reject the symbolism of John Paul II's presence and his blessing when he travels. Some of the key symbols that endure from this papacy teach more powerfully than all the words. Let us remember seven of these:

▷ the first ever visit of a pope to the Lutheran church in Rome on the occasion of the five hundredth anniversary of Martin Luther's birth

▷ the pope's visit to Gandhi's tomb

▷ and to Hiroshima

▷ the visit to Auschwitz with the pope kneeling in prayer

▷ the papal visit to the Jewish Synagogue in Rome where he participated in a prayer service

▷ the embrace between the Bishop of Rome and the Ecumenical Patriarch of Constantinople

▷ the prayer service with representatives of world religions at Assisi

These symbols count the most. They unify the church and they appeal to conscience. They lead people not by words which exclude them but by symbols which embrace them. Symbols lead people to meditative reflection and bring them into the interior of their being.

As a new millennium approaches, I regret the fact that this pope did not use symbols more often. The words got in the way of the symbols. The magisterial teaching distanced people rather than inviting them into the heart of the church. I wish he had used his travels to tell the world and the church how much the church needs forgiveness for its failures and how ardently the church wishes to become a light for the world by example and insight. I believe that no one in the world can make this witness as powerfully as the pope can.

Let me create a scenario to make my point. Consider the symbolism and the power if the pope made only fourteen trips in his pontificate, each of them a global station of the cross, instructing wordlessly, asking for forgiveness symbolically, inviting the whole world into collaboration and compassion.

FIRST STATION: CONSTANTINOPLE
Theme: Forgiveness for the Crusades and for the Division of East and West.

SECOND STATION: WITTENBERG AT LUTHER'S TOMB
Theme: Forgiveness for the Separation of Rome and the Protestant churches of the Reformation.

THIRD STATION: JERUSALEM
Theme: Forgiveness for forgetting the compassion of Jesus by conducting the Inquisitions and persecuting theologians.

FOURTH STATION: NAZARETH
Theme: Forgiveness for denigrating family life by refusing a married priesthood and by forbidding divorce and remarriage in all cases.

FIFTH STATION: ROUEN
Theme: Forgiveness for the way women have been dishonored, at the place where Joan of Arc was burned.

SIXTH STATION: WASHINGTON, DC.
Theme: Forgiveness for condemning democracy, rejecting the separation of church and State, and censuring religious freedom.

SEVENTH STATION: FLORENCE
Theme: Forgiveness at the tomb of Galileo for the persecution and vilification of scientists.

EIGHTH STATION: MEXICO CITY
Theme: Forgiveness for the missionary zealotry which
condoned the enslavement and death of Native Americans
and indigenous people around the world.

NINTH STATION: DELHI
Theme: Proclamation of the goodness of all religions
in India where the oldest world religion emerged.

TENTH STATION: HIROSHIMA
Theme: Proclamation that the church stands for
the ecological health of the planet and for further reflection on
means to responsible parenthood.

ELEVENTH STATION: PARIS AT THE UNIVERSITY OF PARIS
Theme: Proclamation that the church endorses academic
freedom and free inquiry in all universities.

TWELFTH STATION: BRASILIA
Theme: Proclamation of liberation theology and
small faith communities as a call of the Spirit in our day

THIRTEENTH STATION: CAIRO
Theme: Forgiveness for the church's complicity in the exploita-
tion of Africa and the church's approval of slavery

FOURTEENTH STATION: MONTECASSINO
Theme: Celebration of monasticism and the spiritual
life the church endorses for all people

Such trips would surely show the Pope to be a Catholic
Pope, a Pope for all people, the only religious world leader, so
to speak, who can focus global attention on a truly planetary,
catholic, comprehensive commitment to creating a new world
in a new millennium with a new spirit.

These trips would end in Rome where an Ecumenical
Council would have on its agenda the themes symbolized by
the global stations of the cross:

▷ the reunion of East and West

▷ the reconciliation of Rome and the Reformers

▷ due process and equity in church law

▷ the ordination of women to the priesthood

▷ optional celibacy

▷ pastoral guidelines for divorce and remarriage

▷ a Constitution for the church and a new structure for it

▷ a Summit of World Religious Leaders Called Regularly

▷ a review of sexual ethics and responsible parenthood

▷ a charter of free inquiry and academic freedom

▷ guidelines on liberation theology
and small faith communities

▷ principles for contemporary spirituality

To move in this direction, by symbol and Council, would rejuvenate the church and bring the gospel to the world with humility and power.

THE POINT OF IT ALL

We have so little faith in ourselves, in people, in the Spirit, in Christ, in God.

So little faith!

We have explored together Cathedral and, especially, Conscience or so–called Cafeteria Catholicism.

In reality, we are seeking more than Catholicism in our search. We reach for all humanity. Conscience is a key element of bonding in this search. The world may not accept Catholicism, but it does respect conscience. It may not want cathedrals but it always finds room for the human heart. It may be weary of all our words but it pays attention to our authentic symbols and deeds.

The Second Vatican Council told us the church is a mystery and that all believers are a pilgrim people. By what right do church officers declare foreclosure on the mystery and the termination of the pilgrimage? Indeed the mystery and the pilgrimage lead us into the midst of the entire human family and into the life of God.

It is there that we find our center.

One cannot build the City of God with cathedrals only. The City of God is built not with stones but with hearts of flesh and life. The Cornerstone of the Cathedral that is rejected becomes often the foundation of a Temple of Easter glory. When the Cathedral is destroyed, a new Temple of conscience and the Spirit is built by more than human hands.

Institutions have shorter life spans than communities. There have been communities of life or families of love from the very beginning. Institutions serve life and do not substitute for it. Religions preach love but communities of people practice it and make it work.

And so our fundamental question in the church should not be about whether something is Catholic but whether it is healthy and holy and human. For if it is all of these, then, it is Catholic also.

GALILEO'S TELESCOPE

JOHN'S WINDOW
A Reflection on the Modern World

I t is not healthy to live and work in one world and to believe and pray in another. The harmony of these two worlds is an issue in the development of a contemporary spirituality.

TWO MILLENNIA AND FIVE CENTURIES

Gospel, church and world are three pivotal points in the church's life over its first two millennia. The gospel dominates the first five centuries as the canon of Scripture, the creeds and Christology are formulated. The sixth to the fifteenth centuries are engaged with the church, its structure, councils, sacraments, judicial system and religious institutions. The last five centuries are concerned with the autonomy of the world and the discovery of its own sacred character. Let us focus on this latter period, an epoch beginning with the discovery of the new world in 1492 and leading to the birth of the new Europe some 500 years later. The task of the twenty–first century, I believe, will be an integration of gospel, church and world. The present crisis in the church derives from the lack of such a synthesis. Each of these last five centuries might be illustrated by choosing a person or event to represent it

BEGINNING...COLUMBUS 1492

Columbus overcame the limited vision of the planet by finding, within the very world he thought he knew, a new world. This led Europe and the church to redefine their sense of the planet's center and it revealed that there was more to the world than they supposed. The world after Columbus was more difficult for the church to control. It manifested its integrity independently of the church's sense of it.

The new world resisted defining itself in terms of monarchy; it saw the secular order as valuable in its own right, separated church and State, inaugurated national democracies, fused together ethnic, racial and religious groups, and generated pragmatic as well as liberation theologies. The world was forever different after Columbus and more autonomous than it was before him.

THE SIXTEENTH CENTURY...LUTHER

If Columbus redesigned the world in the fifteenth century, Luther redefined the church in the sixteenth century Columbus helped us to see that the center of the world was not where people supposed it was. Luther shifted the center of the church from the papacy to the New Testament, from the hierarchy to people, from sacraments to conscience, from authority to consensus. Luther called for a new relationship with the world, one which saw marriage as a good in itself and not as a concession to human weakness, one which expanded the notion of vocation to include not only clerical callings but worldly tasks. To be a lay person in Luther's church was to exist in a fully privileged state of life, not inferior to ordained pastors; a lay person could be wholeheartedly a citizen of the world and need not go to a monastery or join the clergy to enhance one's relationship with God. The world was different after Columbus; it began to be seen as sacred after Luther.

THE SEVENTEENTH CENTURY...GALILEO

It was especially with Galileo that the world took on a different significance. Galileo somehow makes the world both sacred and insignificant. It is sacred because it is addressed in its own terms. It is insignificant because the world is no longer the stationary center of the solar system. Galileo does not yet have the key of how to endow the world with significance again. Einstein will show us that the relationship of the insignificant to everything else in the cosmos is what makes it significant.

"Truth", Galileo declares in Bertolt Brecht's play, "is the daughter of Time, not of Authority." Authority, we might observe, adds nothing to Truth; it is Truth which gives moral force to Authority. Truth is larger than the church. The church only proclaims the Truth effectively if it learns first how to serve the Truth. In the case of Galileo, the church demands that the Truth be judged in the church's terms, as though the Truth were smaller than the church.

The drama between Galileo and the Inquisition is heightened by the tension between the validity of human experience and the demands of those who dismiss data which displease them.

Brecht's play, *Galileo* reminds us: "You can't make a man unsee what he has seen."

Galileo, unfortunately, gives in to the Inquisition. He consoles himself with the thought that "There is no such thing as a scientific work only one man can write. " When his disappointed colleagues speak of how sad a land is when it has no heroes Galileo replies: "Unhappy is the land that needs a hero".

A church that requires one man to write its theology and set its policies, a church which needs only one man to be a hero in it, is an unhappy church. If theology is Truth, then anyone can write it. The Truth is compelling in its own right; it does not have to be obligatory. If the church is a healthy community, then it needs no hero; its own life is the heroic deed and all its members are the heroic gesture. A family does not need a hero; it needs love and forgiveness and relationship so that all its members come to believe they are valued.

Galileo once asked a persistent critic of his, Giulio Libri, a philosopher at the University of Pisa, to come to Florence and look through the telescope. Libri replied that there was no need to do so because he knew the truth already.

In 1600, Rome burned to death the Dominican Friar Giordano Bruno for teaching that the earth moves. Ten years later, Galileo published the same thesis and proved with his telescope that the world was different from the church's definition of it. In 1633, Galileo, threatened with torture and death, capitulated to the Inquisition. He remained a prisoner, despite his recantation, until his death in 1642.

All the world knows this: it was not Galileo Rome imprisoned but a truth it could not control and could not make less than itself.

It has been said that Galileo shouted out in moral triumph "Eppur si muove". The earth moves and Rome cannot stop it. It moves because the world is sacred, with its own integrity and meaning, regardless of what Rome says of it. The truth is not made in Rome. Before the truth, Rome is a servant, the servant of the servants of God.

Rome can no longer be the immovable center of an ecclesiastical solar system. It cannot sit in judgment of Columbus and Luther and Galileo; it must relate to them and move with them and learn from them and correct its errors and become a mobile part rather than the immutable center of reality.

The truth cannot be arrested in its forward movement or confined in the prison of lesser worlds.

THE EIGHTEEN CENTURY...
THE AMERICAN REVOLUTION

As one moves into the Eighteenth Century, one must become delicate with one's choices. The sacredness and autonomy of the world are accelerating. The world's value is proclaimed not only by Galileo but also by the Renaissance and the Enlightenment, not only by the American Revolution but also by the French Revolution. The Truth is seen as something which abides in the world as it does in the church, in the minds of human beings as readily as it does in the magisterium, in the texture of everyday life as surely as it does in the texts of Scripture. When modern people wish to have their experience validated or the Truth tested, they go, not to the church first, but to the world

Truth is now clearly seen as the daughter of Time rather than of Authority. It is not the work of one person, even a pope, or of one institution, even the church, but the collaborative and collegial work of the entire human family.

The Truth, like the Risen Christ, is not obliged to reveal itself in the Temple or even in the priesthood. Like the Risen Christ, the Truth may appear anywhere. It is not the task of the beholder to predict or to control the appearance but to recognize its validity. The disciples had no authority to proclaim Easter and needed none. They were convincing because they themselves were convinced; it was what they saw and experienced which they proclaimed; they were imprisoned by a religious system for their convictions. They did not fear open debate or disagreement but religious leaders of their time did.

As one enters the Eighteenth Century, the work of Columbus, Luther and Galileo are seen to be essentially correct. Perhaps I might be forgiven the choice of the American Revolution as the representative event for this century. I make this choice partly because I am an American, more substantially because it succeeded, I would argue, in keeping church and world in friendly alliance even though the Revolution made the church and world separate, liberating the world from a need to be defined by the church.

In any case, allow me to say that the American Revolution was a strong protest, not against a Europe-centered World (which Columbus shattered) nor against an oppressive papal center for the church (which Luther shattered) nor against an earth-centered cosmos (which Galileo shattered) but against a monarch-centered nation (which the American Revolution shattered).

The American Revolution returns the nation to people just as Luther returned to the church to the laity. Like Columbus, it had no maps to this new world of national democracy and constitutional limits. It built its new structures from observation and experiment, as Galileo did, and it defined the Truth in its own integrity without seeking the church's endorsement. Legitimacy would come not from the church but from the electorate, now seen capable of validating the Truth from the work of the Spirit, if you will, in its midst. America trusted people as Luther once trusted the laity.

If Columbus changed the geography of the world and Luther, the definition of the church and Galileo, the boundaries of the solar system, the American Revolution changed the constitution of the political order in the modern world. The Bill of Rights declares the autonomy and sacredness of the human person; checks and balances restrict the ability of one minister of government to define Truth as the daughter of its own authority.

In all of this, I do not wish to give America more than its due nor do I suggest that there was not a dark side to the American Revolution and its aftermath. Nonetheless, the world is profoundly different and autonomous after the American Revolution as it was after Columbus, Luther and Galileo.

THE NINETEENTH CENTURY...DARWIN

My choice of Darwin is not done without competitors. Marx and Freud are also candidates. I choose Darwin because the work of Marx and Freud may be less clearly correct in as many of its parts. In any case, this is not a comprehensive paper nor one immune to challenge and improvement. It is my intent to discern patterns and dynamics rather than to achieve universal agreement or to exclude alternative possibilities.

Darwin's thought will be condemned by the church as was the American separation of church and State. Eppur si muove. The Truth goes on even when Authority calls a halt to its march through time. Since Truth is not Authority's daughter, Authority has no parental rights or moral influence over it.

In Darwin, human biology is freed to pursue its own autonomy or Truth since it has not been set rigidly by God but formed, almost capriciously, by Time. The church's ability to base its ethics on the absoluteness of human biology is dealt a severe blow by Darwin. The church will reject the data once again without examination and will declare in the twentieth century that human biology, seen as absolute and unchangeable, predetermines the ethical judgment on contraception and abortion, artificial insemination, in vitro fertilization, and the right to die. All of these realities are supposedly resolved by the priority of human biology over human choice, indeed by making human biology the immovable center of an ethical solar system, if you will. Once again, the church declares it has no need to look through the telescope. All of these issues, Rome declares, are settled in advance and without exception. Indeed, the sovereignty of human biology is invoked to define the ethics of homosexuality and even to dictate whether women may be ordained to the priesthood. I am not saying that Rome is incorrect in all these instances, though it may well be, but I am suggesting that Rome is working again with the wrong solar system.

In the nineteenth century, church representatives declared that human biology was not developed from lower forms of life, that it existed in splendid isolation from them and that the church knew this with certainty. In a previous century, the church had declared that the earth was the center of the solar system and that it knew this with certainty.

One is astonished, in the light of how often the church was simply wrong in the modern era at its audacity in proclaiming papal infallibility. It could only do this effectively under a Pope, Pius IX, who rejected the entire modern world and its political order as evil and who sought to control the Truth in a papal center. Pius IX did this in the *Syllabus of Errors* before calling the First Vatican Council to define his infallibility.

THE TWENTIETH CENTURY...EINSTEIN

With Einstein, we come to understand that the universe has no center and that interrelationship is what holds the whole of reality together.

It has been said that we pattern our lives on the models of the universe our culture gives us. There have been three models during the two millennia of the church's existence.

The first of these was the Ptolemaic model. It envisioned the universe as an earth-centered reality and arranged the spheres or planets around it in a strict hierarchical order. The empyrean, or the stars, for example, were seen as pure and everlasting; the earth was dark and mortal. We find this model in Dante's *Divina Commedia.*

This model prevailed through the ten centuries, the fifth to the fifteenth, when the structure of the hierarchical church was put in place. The pope and bishops existed in splendid isolation from the rest of the church; they had direct communication with God and were sacred personages in a way the laity, unless they were royal, were not. This Ptolemaic universe gave us a Ptolemaic Papacy.

The second of these models was the Newtonian model. It was developed after Galileo by Isaac Newton. It is a heliocentered system dominated not by hierarchical spheres but by absolute clarity and translucent mathematical laws. All is in movement but nothing is in doubt; everything is mechanistically determined in a clock-work, impersonal universe. This model prevails during the sixteenth to the twentieth centuries.

These centuries give us what I would call a Newtonian Magisterium. The church now accelerates the development of a teaching authority in which everything can be settled, clarified and resolved in the church's terms. There is to be one model theology for the church, one form of worship, one canon law, one approved catechism, one celibate priesthood. The Newtonian Magisterium eventually declares itself infallible. The question raised now in the church, especially among the bishops, is not whether what the pope says is true or even useful but whether the pope has decided to teach infallibly or not. Certitude and clarity are seen as primary values; doubt and ambiguity are considered weaknesses. When Paul VI issues *Humanae Vitae* which is, after all, only an encyclical and not a Council, the question raised anxiously in the church was whether this teaching was infallible or not, clear and final for all time or whether Catholics were permitted to discuss it. John Paul 11 appoints bishops whose teaching on all matters of church doctrine and discipline is to be unambiguously clear. The Newtonian Magisterium is certain, unbending, mechanistic, impersonal, and unreachable. Truth is no longer the daughter of Time but of Authority.

Einstein gives us a third model, a universe relative and relational in all its parts, participatory in every instance. Every atom influences every other so that nothing exists in isolation. There is no hierarchy; the universe is catholic and universal. There is no clarity; the universe is a profound mystery and we stand in awe before it.

The only Ecumenical Council held since Einstein, Vatican II, is a Council which reflects this. It calls for collegiality and community, declares none of its teaching infallible and gives us participatory images of the church as the People of God and the Liturgy as the work of the priesthood of all believers. It tells us the church is a mystery and calls for a community of local churches with different cultures, theologies and traditions. Vatican 11 is vastly different from the Ptolemaic Papacy of an Innocent III for example. It does not require, as Vatican I did, Newtonian clarity, papal infallibility and rational certitude to make its point.

In Einstein's universe, all is in movement and nothing is at rest. If movement could stop for an instant, the universe would end. "I move, therefore, I am," one might say.

It is foolish in such a context to continue obligatory celibacy only because we have done this for a long time or to reaffirm the prohibition of contraception because change might confuse people. It is unconvincing to deny the ordination of women because we have not ordained women in the past.

Change, in Einstein's universe, is not frantic but creative; all is held in check by its relationship to everything else. Einstein tells us that the universe has a shape but no center and that no part gives direction and purpose to all the other parts.

By theological application, we might maintain that God does not exist in any center but is somehow everywhere. There is no privileged place to be; it is a privilege just to be. And God is fully there. All parts of the body are fully alive, no one part more alive than any other. Indeed, it is the whole body which is alive as all its parts come together so that the body is somehow less a body when a part is missing.

Einstein put the separate pieces of the universe together and showed how they relate to one another. He joined light to time and time to space and space to gravity and energy to matter. As he did this, he gave us the dynamics which would lead to Vatican II. John XXIII opened a window and looked through Galileo's telescope and called a Council. And so, now, we seek to join the papacy to the bishops and bishops to people and priests to community and authority to conscience and sacred to secular and gospel to world and Christianity to other religions and Catholicism to Orthodoxy and Protestantism and male to female and America to Europe and Socialism to Capitalism and stability to change and marriage to priesthood.

Our voyage is to a new world, sometimes without maps but never without one another, always with a measure of fear but not without hope, able to recognize a new continent in the pale October moonlight of 1492 or a new church in the open window of October 1962, when Vatican II begins. Our voyage is through the broken Berlin Wall and beyond Tienanman Square and it enlists the free hearts of former Soviet citizens and the free spirit which now brings all of Europe together. Our companions on this journey are the people we love and the children we bear, the dreams we fashion in darkness and the prayers we formulate at dawn, the commitments we choose and the love we make and the tears we shed and the songs we sing.

Only a static church in a changing universe could deny all this life or seek to punish it. Had the church had its way Luther and Galileo and democracy and evolution would all have perished. The static church would prefer that we look to the infallible papacy to settle all questions about the church and the solar system, about the priesthood of all believers and the origin of the species, about the separation of church and State and even the issues we may publicly debate. In a universe of infinite majesty and movement, a Ptolemaic Papacy and a Newtonian Magisterium are quaint and inert.

JOHN'S WINDOW

Cardinal Barberini was a friend of Galileo and receptive to Galileo's ideas. When he became Pope Urban VIII, however, he threatened Galileo with torture until he recanted and denied the validity of his data. How could Urban VIII have done this to a .friend whose theories, he realized, were persuasive?

In his play, *Galileo*, Bertolt Brecht gives us a plausible solution. Brecht portrays Urban VIII discussing the Galileo case with the Cardinal Inquisitor. During their conversation, the pope attires for a ceremony. Before he vests, he is open to Galileo. As each vestment is put on him, he becomes more hostile. When he is fully vested, he finds torture acceptable.

Brecht shows us a pope who lives and works in one world, who believes and prays in another. Urban VIII denies the validity of his own experience for the demands of an institution and his own position in it. Truth is the casualty in this denial of evidence.

Galileo and Urban VIII are separated by the papacy and by their choice to live in two different solar systems. In Galileo's system, truth is not discovered by authority but in time; human experience, the world's autonomy and intellectual concerns are seen as convincing. In Urban's system, truth is made by authority; human experience, the world and the intellect are subordinate.

In our lifetime, a very different pope, John XXIII, opened a window and the Second Vatican Council in 1962. He declared in the inaugural speech at the Council that "violence inflicted on others" gives us "no help at all in finding a happy solution to" our problems. The Second Vatican in *Gaudium et Spes* described the world as meaningful in its own right; it saw marriage as a relationship of life and love and it discovered God in the signs of the times.

Out of these correlations and connections an utterly new spirituality will be generated, one which derives as much from the world as it does from the gospel, as much from the personality of each person as it does from the church and its tradition. As believers move into this new universe, they will discover that it has no center; the center will be created where life happens intensely and where it maintains a relationship with other life.

This spirituality will not develop from general principles enunciated by a universal church in some theoretical manner but from those passionate experiences which move the human heart profoundly and take it beyond itself. It is only when we feel our humanity move to its depths, to its point of exhaustion and transcendence, that we encounter Christ. It is passion which breaks the human heart open so that God can enter. Doctrine and theology, sacral institutions and legal systems, as such, do not do this, especially when they alienate us from our identities and compel us to live in a world whose center and solar systems are artificial and contrived. The reason why so much church teaching is irrelevant is because it is written for a world which does not exist anymore and is addressed to lives which have not yet found their own center.

It is noteworthy that the disciples in the gospels do not find

Jesus in the Temple. They discover Jesus as they work in the open fields and on turbulent seas. They encounter Jesus where they experience life. In the Pastoral Epistles we are instructed to choose our church leaders only from those who have made a passionate commitment to one woman and who have entered deeply into family life. The early church was a domestic church and its ritual was the celebration of a family meal. It did not need the Temple to make it holy. Its sanctity came from the memories and hopes one brought to the meal, from the love and passion with which life was shared, and from the spirit of God which became present to all this. The early church needed little structure to sustain it; wherever two or three gathered, the church became possible and Christ was present. We must not, of course, romanticize this early church so that we see it as having no problems. We cite it only because its priorities seem to have been better than ours.

In this early assembly of Christians, Peter was still a fisherman and Paul a tent maker; apostles had families and the gathering of the community made the Eucharist happen. It was important to know the faces and names around the table because the Eucharist did not depend upon the priesthood even less upon celibacy, but upon the community and the memories, hopes, passions and lives of those who gathered.

When Einstein gave us a limitless model for the universe and when John XXIII opened a window, our hearts and souls were exposed to all the agony and ecstasy of our concrete lives. Confusion may follow as we enter this new world and restructure our lives so that they fit our times. We may indeed experience a dark night of the soul. The dark night of the soul is the act by which we fall from a lesser truth to a greater truth. The greater truth is a unified world in which we can live and work and pray and believe. We can no longer return to a world which subjects truth to obedience or passion to an institution or conscience to law. We wish no more to do this now than the disciples of Jesus wished to become Temple priests. They preferred to break bread in the open fields and in the warmth of their own homes and families. We have learned well what the early disciples knew, namely, that the human heart and

51

the real world must not be denied since God abides preeminently in them.

CODA

As we complete these reflections, let us keep in mind the images which unified them: Columbus' flagship and Luther's ninety-five theses, Galileo's telescope and the American Bill of Rights, Darwin's organic connections and Einstein's open-ended equations. All of these images were formed in passion and vibrated with life so abundant that it could not be contained in the old wineskins of lesser truths and visions.

Nothing less than God and Truth are at issue in all this. The universe and the new church bring with them the new Christ who bursts open the confinements of lesser worlds and restrictive church systems. The Risen Christ is less clearly defined than the historical Jesus but we feel this Christ more passionately in our hearts. The first disciples did not find the Risen Christ in the Temple. He came to them as they worked on the seas again and when they gathered as a family in the Upper Room. The New Christian church seemed worldly to the traditional Jewish establishment. It appeared outrageous as it extended the priesthood to all believers.

But the spirit compelled the disciples ever forward, into the whole world, beyond Jerusalem, into a limitless universe. There they found their mission.

A MEDITATION ON MEMORY *&* HOPE

Building a Future

Allow me to take you back 500 years to the summer of 1492. Come with me to Spain, to Italy, to Germany. When we complete this reflection, we may be able to deal better with the present crisis in the church, a crisis in which, as we shall see, ecclesiology, ministry and spirituality are at issue.

On Friday, August 3, 1492, before dawn, a 41 year old man, set sail out of Palos, Spain, with three ships and a crew of ninety men. He headed for what we call the Atlantic Ocean; his contemporaries had named it the "Sea of Darkness." In the description of an Arab geographer it was a sea of profound darkness, high waves, frequent storms, monsters, and violent winds. To direct one's ships in such a direction required uncommon courage and extraordinary imagination. We are speaking, of course, of Christopher Columbus. The terror we have already indicated was intensified by the likelihood that the crew would starve to death before it reached land. In retrospect, we know they would have had the unknown continent of America not been there. It could have taken Columbus over six months to reach Japan, his original destination, rather than the 36 days of the actual crossing.

By late September of 1492, there was panic aboard the *Santa Maria*. The log of Columbus records the agreement of the crew on

October 10 to sail for no more than three days and then return to Spain if land were not found. At 2:00 a.m., in the pale moonlight of October 12, a sailor on the Pinta cried out in disbelief and exuberance "Tierra! Tierra."

We are aware of the ambiguities with which we recall this event or encounter between Europe and America. I wish to focus, however, on a fact we can all accept. The world and the church were forever changed by this moment of history. The new world, then and now, challenged the categories and presuppositions of European culture and theology.

Now, let us travel to Italy, more specifically to Rome. It is still the summer of 1492. Columbus left Spain on Friday, August 3, as we have said. Eight days later, at a conclave in Rome, on Saturday, August 11, a new pope is elected. As the counting of the ballots makes it obvious that the new pope will be Rodrigo Borgia, a Spaniard, another Cardinal, Giovanni de' Medici cries out "Flee, we are in the hands of a wolf." With a fleet of Spanish ships under sail to encounter a new world and a Spanish pope, newly elected, we might say 1492 was the year of Spain.

We need to put the papacy in context in the fifteenth century before we can understand the cry in the conclave that the new pope is a wolf.

As the fifteenth century began, there were three popes: Benedict XIII, Gregory XII, and John XXIII. At the University of Paris, 10,000 student signatures had been collected, asking the popes to resign and calling for an Ecumenical Council.

Finally, on November 1, 1414, a Council is called by one of the three popes. It is to assemble in Germany, the only Ecumenical Council ever to take place there. The pope who is forced to call this Council of Reform and Reunion is John XXIII. As we shall see, a little over 500 years later, another John XXIII will call a Council of Reform and Reunion in 1962.

The first John XXIII is forced to call an Ecumenical Council to end the shameful schism into which the three popes have led the Catholic church. He does not want a Council and relents only when he is told that if the Council takes place without his convoking it, it will put him on trial for murder, rape, sodomy and incest. The pope agrees to call the Council and to resign.

Finally, on November 1, 1414, the Catholic world breathes free. The Council convenes in Constance and the three popes resign. In the wake of the failure of the papacy, an Ecumenical Council will rescue the church.

Why do I mention all this? I do this for two reasons:

▷ Catholics must not be ignorant of their own history

▷ One cannot understand the present reform movement in the Catholic church and its call for a renewed spirituality and ministry without seeing that opposition to official papal policy is not necessarily a sign of disloyalty to the church, to the papacy, or to Christ

Let us, however, return to Germany and the Council of Constance. The Council of Constance met from 1414-1418. It issued two of the most important decrees in modem church life. Had these two decrees been followed, there never would have been a Reformation and the Council would have saved the church again.

One of these decrees, *Haec Sancta*, approved on April 6, 1415, declared the preeminence of an Ecumenical Council to a pope as Catholic doctrine. It reads as follows:

> *"all princes of whatever rank or dignity, even the pope, are bound to obey the Council in matters relating to faith and the end of this schism and the general reformation of the church."*

By 1417, the Council is ready to elect a new pope. The legitimacy of the modem papacy will depend upon the validity of this Council and on its right to dismiss popes when they mislead the church.

Immediately before the election, the Council passes a second, crucial document and elects the new pope on the basis of it. The document, *Frequens* is passed on October 9, 1417, a century earlier than the Reformation (October 31, 1517). The date is seventy four years earlier, almost to the day, of the arrival of Columbus' ships at San Salvador in the Bahamas, October 12, 1492.

What did *Frequens* have to say? It obliged all popes to call Councils at regular intervals whether they chose to or not. The Councils would serve as a way of keeping popes accountable and preserving the church from schism.

About a month after this decree is passed, a new pope, Martin V (Oddo Colonna), is elected on November 11, 1417.

Allow me to make a point about the present before I return to the past. There were two issues which pope Paul VI refused to allow Vatican II to discuss. One of these was birth control and the other was whether obligatory celibacy should be terminated. He assumed that the papacy could solve these issues better, on its own, without the Council. Vatican II closed in 1965; Paul VI reaffirmed obligatory celibacy in an encyclical, *Sacerdotalis Caelibatus* in 1967 and reaffirmed the prohibition against artificial birth control in another encyclical, *Humane Vitae,* in 1968. These issues bear more on the development of contemporary spirituality and ministry than most realize because they touch on issues of sexuality and the role of women, the dignity of marriage and questions of power in the church with an immediacy and force which we must not underestimate. The prohibition of artificial birth control brings with it a suspicion about human sexuality that makes it difficult for the official church to see sexual experience as sacramental and relational. I submit further that a church cannot insist on obligatory celibacy for its pastoral leaders without also teaching, at least by implication, that marriage is an inferior Christian vocation.

I suggest furthermore that had the pope allowed the Council to consider these issues, it would have given better guidance. The quiet and unofficial schism which has gone on in the church, a schism which leads 90% of the Catholic laity to reject the teaching on artificial birth control, a schism which has led to the resignation of 125,000 priests in the last 25 years and left almost half of all

58

Catholic parishes world-wide without pastors, such a quiet schism, draining the heart and energy and vitality of the church, such a schism I submit would not have occurred. If the Council dealt with these issues it would have approved of artificial birth control as the subsequent papal commissions and a number of the national episcopal letters after *Humane Vitae,* in effect, did. The Council would have allowed the ordination of married men at least in mission countries.

Let us return to the fifteenth century for a few more comments and then we shall discuss the present in its own right. We might note, however, that by discussing the past I am already addressing the present

Some twenty years after the Council of Constance, the one and only Council ever held in Florence, Italy occurs. The year is 1438. The Council has as one of its major goals the healing of the split between Eastern Orthodoxy and the Latin West. The East believes this is now possible because the Council of Constance has taught that the Catholic church is not a papal church but a conciliar church. It had defined itself as a church in which the body of bishops is more than any one bishop even if he be the Bishop of Rome. It had, furthermore, preserved the papacy as a crucial and central office in the church but as one subject to accountability by other structures in the church.

Bishops from both East and West considered Florence the eighth rather than the sixteenth Ecumenical Council (as the West counted). This is very significant and gives us an insight into what, I believe, will occur in the future.

East and West were able to call this the eighth council because the Councils of the second millennium, after the split between Constantinople and Rome, were not full Councils of the church and, therefore, not truly Ecumenical. The first seven Councils, perhaps, the greatest ever held, were open to East and West, even though few Westerners came to them. These Councils invited the five major patriarchs of the Catholic church, including the Patriarch of the West, the Bishop of Rome. Indeed, the West through the centuries, including later Protestant Reformers, affirmed these seven Councils as Ecumenical and in the affirmation had a voice and a vote, so to speak, in them.

The next eight Councils, however, excluded the East explicitly and the four other patriarchs from Jerusalem, Antioch, Alexandria, and Constantinople. Furthermore, they were never affirmed by the East or considered by them Ecumenical. These eight councils were the first to be called by the pope alone and were, in effect, Councils of the West.

The first seven councils were called by laity, albeit emperors. Indeed, the first Council, Nicaea, on which the Catholic doctrine of the Trinity and Christology rests, was called by a non–Christian layman, the not yet baptized Constantine. History allows us to see new possibilities for the church, does it not? These seven Councils are considered the greatest, even though the pope neither called them nor attended them.

It was in the last eight councils before Florence, running from First Lateran in 1123 to Constance in 1414-1418 that the papacy assumed total control of the church. These were the Councils which brought in obligatory celibacy, prohibited remarriage after divorce (permitted until then), codified church law, called Crusades, sanctioned Inquisitions. These Councils declared that henceforth only the pope could call a Council.

After Florence, a Council at Trent created the Index of Forbidden Books and made the pope and hierarchy almost divine so that to be against the pope was somewhat like being against the church, Jesus Christ, and God.

I do not wish to suggest that many good things were not occurring through these centuries. One cannot say everything in one essay. Certainly, Francis of Assisi, Dominic, Ignatius, Teresa of Avila, John of the Cross, great religious communities, an enhanced role for woman, courageous missionaries, saintly popes, Meister Eckhart, Catherine of Siena, the great cathedrals and universities, the mighty monasteries, Joan of Arc, pilgrimages and Marian devotion, Bernard of Clairvaux and Julian of Norwich, the list could go on and on. All these attest to something true about the Catholic church then and now, namely, that it never loses the gospel and that it inspires people with Christ so that their whole heart is taken by him. It remains a church of enormous creativity and grace, with a potential to reach the world matched, perhaps, by no other Christian church. Had I dwelt only on these issues, however, I would not have the opportunity to address adequately the crisis of spirituality and ministry.

We were speaking about the Council of Florence and I digressed. I was saying that a number of Latin bishops agreed to call Florence the eighth ecumenical council. I had said this was significant. I did not say why.

I believe that early in the third millennium, a great Council will be called with bishops from the East and West invited as full members and all having equal votes. It will declare itself the eighth or the ninth Council, the last full council having been Nicaea II, called in 787. I submit it will declare all the Councils of the second millennium, all the Councils called by popes, all the Councils giving the pope full control of the church and declaring him infallible, it will declare those Councils partial Councils, not fully Ecumenical, because the East was not invited. It will be, I predict, a great Council and it will preserve a permanent role for the Bishop of Rome but it will not submit the entire church to his approval.

As I leave this topic, I wish to note that the seventh Council, Nicaea II, was called by a Catholic laywoman, the Empress Irene. She presided over its sessions and approved its decrees.

We are still in the fifteenth century. Columbus is on his way to a new world. The cardinals gather in conclave to elect a new pope. They are aware that only 74 years before, the Council of Constance had forced popes to resign and that only 50 years earlier, in 1442, the Council of Florence had finished its work and almost united East and West.

Rodrigo Borgia has just been elected. He will publicly recognize all seven of his illegitimate children and continue to live with his two mistresses, Vanozza and Giulia. He will take the name of Alexander VI and create an era of unparalleled corruption continuing through his successors Julius II and Leo X, until Europe, unable to call a reform Council without the pope and despairing of hopes for renewal, will be racked by the Reformation.

On October 31, 1517, a relatively young monk, thirty-four years of age, will call for debate on the papacy and the church. Martin Luther was nine years old when Alexander VI was elected and when Giovanni de' Medici cried out "Flee, we are in the hands of a wolf." He was twenty years old when Alexander VI was dragged to his grave by ropes since no one wanted to touch the body of a man people claimed had sold his soul to the devil. Martin Luther was in his twenties as Alexander's successor, pope Julius 11, rode at the head of the papal armies and declared that he loved battle and bloodshed. Erasmus of Rotterdam, a moderate Catholic reformer, writes in *Praise of Folly* (1509): "How dare you, Bishop [of Rome], you who hold the place of the Apostle, how dare you school your people in war?" Luther is in his early thirties as pope Leo X declares "God has given us the papacy. Let us enjoy it" and as Leo orders the strangling of a cardinal who had tried to poison the pope.

Luther cries out: "Enough! In the name of God, enough. We are not justified by popes or indulgences but by Jesus Christ and our faith in him. If the pope can empty Purgatory by granting indulgences for a price, why does he not empty it out of love? If the pope allows people to enter heaven, do we need Christ anymore?"

And, so, the fifteenth century comes to a close. In the summer of 1492, Columbus sails for a new world, people remember the scandal of three popes simultaneously claiming legitimacy for themselves, as well as the Councils of Constance and Florence. The hearts of many Christians sink in despair as Alexander VI assumes the papacy.

THE PRESENT

Four hundred years before the Second Vatican Council began (1962), the Council of Trent had opened its final deliberations. The Catholic church in 1962 was very much like the Catholic church of 1562. All this, however, was about to change. Spirituality, ministry and church were dealt with in much the same way from 1562–1962; a radical break with this past was about to occur at the end of the summer in 1962.

What we see in Vatican II is an effort to return, in some way, to the Council of Constance. Constance tried to give us a church of the Ecumenical Council, namely, a church in which many would have a significantly participatory role to play in the formation of church, spirituality and ministry.

Vatican II, however, went much further than this and became one of the most revolutionary Councils in church history.

Orthodox Christianity believes that a Council becomes infallible not when the bishops declare it to be so but over the centuries as people affirm the Council and follow or reject its teaching by their behavior and convictions. If we apply this norm to Vatican II, we might ask which teaching of the Council people have assimilated most profoundly. We can do this by looking at the six documents which have engaged the church most creatively over the last thirty years. The other ten documents of Vatican II have had considerably less impact.

The premier teaching of Vatican II resides in its Constitution on the church, *Lumen Gentium*. In the summer of 1962 we continued to call the church a perfect society and we limited the laity to a role of participating in the apostolate of the hierarchy. Authority was seen as a pyramid, dissent was equivalent to spiritual corruption, "ministry" was a Protestant word, ordained priests were considered greater than the angels and, indeed, "other Christs", the world was an evil place to be, its schools and universities a danger to the faith, its substantial investment in marriage and family an example of secular rather than sacred living. *Lumen Gentium* claimed the church was a mystery far more than a society and that

63

it was preeminently the People of God rather than the hierarchy and its ordained ministers. It defined the laity as a structure in its own right and it called for a spirituality of engagement with the church and world rather than a spirituality of obedience, self-sacrifice, and regret for not being both a celibate and a priest.

In its Constitution on the Church in the Modem World, the Council went further. It defined marriage as a central structure of Christian living and it called the family a domestic church. It described marriage (in the most beautiful Council description of it in history) as a marital community of life and love and as a vocation in which the substance of the church was present. It saw social justice as constitutive of the essence of the church and laid the groundwork for liberation theology and the preferential option for the poor. It viewed sexuality in a new light and disengaged it from a primarily reproductive experience and it called for study on the church's teaching on birth control. In effect, spirituality and ministry became more rooted in this world and in the body seen, of course, in the light of Christ and the gospel.

The revolution continued through the Decree on Ecumenism. as the Catholic church adopted almost every item of Luther's Reformation. It made the Bible central in a way that was unthinkable in the summer of 1962 before the ground breaking Constitution on Revelation was approved and it subordinated the magisterium to the larger realities of both Scripture and Tradition. The Constitution on Revelation created a new context for creative rethinking about Christ and the gospels.

The Constitution on the Liturgy brought the church the most creative liturgical reform in its history- It gave us in the Eucharistic celebration an icon of what the entire church can be and is as it assembles to worship God and celebrate Christ.

In its Declaration on Religious Freedom, the council spoke of conscience and human rights in a way the pre-councilar church would have rejected as individualistic and worldly.

In the years after the Council, the Catholic laity and their pastors received its teaching with the impact of lightening on the road to Damascus, leaving them sometimes blind and confused from the luminosity of the Spirit but also convinced and committed to traveling a very different path in the future.

Paul VI became the first pope to return to Jerusalem and he embraced the Orthodox Ecumenical Patriarch, Athenagoras, there, and later went to the World Council of churches in Geneva to pray with Protestants. Images came in on all sides as Catholics realized that an earthquake and a whirlwind had engulfed the Catholic church and re-arranged almost everything in the ecclesial landscape.

Altars faced the people and priests prayed in the vernacular; women distributed communion and religious orders changed their dress and their constitutions; the clergy gathered in senates and the bishops in national conferences.

One of the most beloved popes of all time, John XXIII, was declared a saint, in effect, not only by Catholics but also by Protestants and Jews. Paul VI addressed the United Nations in New York and cried out unforgettably: "No more war. Never again. No more war. Never again." Catholics refused military service and women religious marched with a Baptist pastor, Martin Luther King, for civil rights. John Paul I refused to wear the papal tiara for his installation as pope. John Paul II knelt in prayer at Hiroshima and at Auschwitz and at Gandhi's grave. Muslims and Christians prayed together at Assisi with Jews and Buddhists and Hindus.

Oscar Romero was slain for preaching liberation and justice for the poor. The revolution was massive, unstoppable, a tidal wave of grace and inspiration. Theresa Kane, a woman religious, asked the pope publicly to rethink his decision on the ordination of women and Catholics proclaimed Luther's preaching as Catholic doctrine. They spoke of a church that must always be reformed ("ecclesia semper reformanda") and of the priesthood of all believers. Married men were ordained deacons and even priests if they were convert pastors.

65

One could continue endlessly in this direction but the point has already been made. Could we return now to the summer of 1962 we would find there a Catholic church we could no longer recognize or accept, a Catholic church so unreal and disengaged from our lives that we would not be able to do ministry effectively in it or find its spirituality vital and creative. This is not to say that all is going well now, how foolish that would be, or that all was misguided then, how shallow that would be. It is merely to say that we have changed forever, at a level and with a force which eludes our imagination and escapes our memory; we have been changed by a new Pentecost of the Spirit and have begun to restructure the church and the ministry and the spiritual life as radically as the early Christians did when the missionary journeys of Paul and the Jerusalem Council called for massive innovations.

We now see the world as good and the church as ours; we now see marriage as a noble gift, equal to celibacy, and, indeed, its complement; we have rediscovered our baptism in the church and pushed the boundaries of the Christian community to include Protestants and even non-Christians; we now see social justice as no less urgent than Liturgy and recognize women as those to whom the church belongs as equally as it does to men. We define our spirituality as less obedient than committed and our ministry as less ecclesial than global. We see the church, not on a pyramid or a military or a corporation model but as a family where disagreement is expected but never a withholding of love.

Of all this we need to be reminded because memory is the substance of hope.

I have found in the last few years across this nation an intensified sense of disappointment with the effort by some to hold back the development of the Spirit of the Council. This disappointment sometimes approximates despair as people resign ministries and leave the church or remain with only half their heart alive and engaged. This has profound effects on spirituality and ministry. It makes it more difficult for most Catholics to see their spirituality as truly ecclesial and forces them to define that spirituality in individualistic terms which they find unsatisfactory.

We affirm the cross but keep hope. The tide will turn whenever it flows too long in the wrong direction. We may be on a Sea of Darkness but the light of a new world is already on the horizon. The prophets of doom, as John XXIII called them, those who think the world is evil and the Council a mistake, the harbingers of gloom who denounce the signs of the times and blame people, democracy and the modem age for all our problems, these do not represent the future.

The future is for those who are confident that both world and church are more graced than they are flawed. Thomas Merton once asked us to ponder the fact that Truth is larger than all of us and it prevails against all odds. We must stop thinking, he noted, that Truth is smaller than we are and so must be safeguarded carefully and belligerently.

It is not October 10, 1492, the day Columbus' ships decided to return to Spain in three days if no land were found. It is rather early morning on October 12. The sky is dark but the moon is full. The light on the shore tells us that the voyage has not been in vain and that there need be no turning back in defeat and despair.

It is not Good Friday in the church but three days later; it is Easter Sunday morning. Every effort to stop the Council has been made. They have all failed. Let us walk now with the brave women who make their way through the early Easter darkness and seek Christ once again. Let us not miss the full Paschal moon in the heavens and the suggestion of a new dawn on the horizon. As we join these women let us recall how near despair they were. And let us also remember that they found in the tomb not the death of all their hopes but more joy and glory than their hearts and even all of history could contain.

POWER,

SEX

&

CHURCH STRUCTURES

Sex and the Roman System

We find Christ on those levels of church life where we encounter compassion. The other levels have little to teach us about Christ. It is very simple. It is counterproductive to qualify, make conditions and excuses, pile up footnotes and cross–references. What are we about as a church anyway? Is it not compassion?

I do not believe that a large institution cannot be compassionate. Vatican II was a compassionate Council; John XXIII was a compassionate pope. Why should they be exceptions? The complex management of a church can be reconciled with compassion. Should it not disturb us that very few think of the word "compassion" when the word Vatican or Roman Catholic is used? The word "gentle" seems far less apt than "powerful" in identifying the Catholic church. Thirty five years ago, with another pope and an impressive Council, "gentle" fit. Some will, no doubt, find flaws in John XXIII's papacy and blind spots in Vatican II. Neither was perfect. But it is the abiding image and memory which matters.

The church is meant to be the Sacrament of God's Compassion. It is called "Mother church" is it not? John XXIII reminded us of this as he opened the Second Vatican Council:

"Mother church rejoices that... the longed–for day has finally dawned...often errors vanish as quickly as they arise, like fog before the sun...the spouse of Christ prefers mercy to severity. She meets the needs of today by witnessing to the goodness of her teaching and not by condemnations...violence inflicted on others...does not help at all in solving the serious problems of the day...the Catholic church...must be a loving mother to all, benign, patient, merciful, doing good to those separated from her.... The Council now beginning rises in the church like day-break, the promise of an even more splendid light. It is now only dawn (but) already (we can) contemplate the stars..."

As I read the gospels, I find Jesus most radical when he addresses two issues: power and sex. Power here is not moral influence over others or even coercive action against evil or even, indeed, genuine authority. Power is oppression, allowing the defenseless and the victims no voice, silencing all those who take their part, fashioning an institution in which the views of one person or a clique determine policy and implement it even against the needs and wishes of the vast majority. This description is not a caricature. It has happened often in world history and is a precise description of what happens in our church from time to time. Let us not evade the issue by making endless qualifications. This power is condemned by Jesus, severely, often. Such power is linked, as I intend to show, with punishment and sexual repression.

It is instructive to observe that once we allow someone to define us primarily by a sexual definition (celibate or married, heterosexual or homosexual, serious sinner or sexually active in a marriage after divorce), once our sexual life becomes the most important way in making a judgment about us, then such a person or institution has gained control of us. It then becomes almost impossible for us to sense our freedom and worth. Totalitarian systems make a great deal of sexual control and use power to enforce it.

Jesus knew this. Hear him when James and John ask for primacy in the Reign of God. He calls the Twelve (symbol of the whole church) to him and says in Mark 10 (paraphrased):

70

"Only pagans when they have no faith seek power. They seek to rule other lives. This is not my way and it is never to be yours. Do you hear? Never. No one of you must rule other lives. For even I held on to none of you with power. I give my life for you. You must do that for one another. Do you hear? No power."

Later he warns, in Mark 12, that we must beware of those who like to walk around in long robes, who seek titles of respect others do not have and who always sit in the best seats in the synagogue and are given places of honor at all banquets. Such people, Jesus thunders, devour widows and plunder the powerless.

The teaching is clear, aimed with deadly force at the hardness of our hearts.

If it is so clear, why do we find it so easy to dismiss it? If the teaching of Jesus is strong in this regard and ambiguous on sexual ethics, why have we made sexual ethics paramount?

The teaching of Jesus on sexual ethics in the gospel is sparse, almost non–existent. This does not indicate there are to be no norms; our sexual behavior can be exploitive and abusive. Jesus knew this. All sensible people do. Why then does Jesus speak so little in this regard?

For Jesus, relationships are pre–eminent because love is the norm for the community. Sex is one way in which we seek permanent relationships. In it, we express love with unique intensity. Power is the way we destroy relationships. In it, we dismiss love as a commodity the system cannot afford.

Is it not noteworthy that people link the word "fidelity" very easily with sexual commitment. The modern world celebrates faithful people and uses the word "faithful' often to describe sexual integrity. The vast majority recognize how deep and painful are the wounds inflicted by sexual betrayals. The world knows this. It does not need many reminders. It learned this on its own.

And, so, Jesus says little about sexuality and is gentle in dealing with sexual misconduct, not because he is unconcerned but precisely because he does not see this as our worst evil. Most people achieve impressive levels of sexual maturity. Why is it so difficult for the church to admit this?

Power, however, is far more devastating.

In the greatest of all parables, the lost son, it is the elder brother, heavily into power, who reminds his father of the sexual misconduct of the son the father has just forgiven. The strategy of the elder son is to crush the younger son with power and to shame him with his sexual behavior. It is easy to shame people with their sexual misdeeds. All tyrants know this. We shame easily about sexual matters because we care so deeply about getting our sexuality right. Sexual responsibility is built into us as a yearning perhaps as deep as our hunger for God. We all need to be assured that our hope for God and our sexual hope for maturity are not in vain.

The forgiving father, in the parable, ignores the sexual charges, much as Jesus does with the woman in adultery. People who make sexual charges against others almost always seek to demean them and then to destroy them.

The father wants to heal and to love the lost son. He does not deny the sexual charges or celebrate the sexual misconduct. He puts it in perspective. It happened. But the son is more than this. And so is the father. The father wants a free son, not a slave kept in parental and sexual bondage forever.

Notice how often right–wing groups and totalitarian systems insist on rigid sexual norms and blind obedience to power.

Anthropologists tell us we have been human for four million years. Christianity has been on the scene for only two thousand years. Was all the previous time a time of no sexual wisdom or maturity? There are a billion Christians now in a world of five billion people. Is there sexual fidelity among all Christians and none in the billions of others? Are the percentages and behaviors markedly different among Christians and others? Do not people, then, even without Christianity, find their way sexually and spiritually? If they do, then why are we so negative in our judgment that Christians can do this as well, without excessive harassment, punishment and intrusion from church leaders.

FROM CHRIST TO MODERNISM

There were many good things which happened after Christ. Our critique always assumes these and is ready to celebrate them. In one talk, one cannot say everything. We must take for granted that there were many glorious moments over two millennia. If we do not accept this, we would not be Catholic. Certainly the monasteries and many church councils, clearly the papacy when it served to unify the Catholic world, undoubtedly the sacramental system, all these, none authorized by Christ, served us well. The centuries are filled with hopeful memories: Benedict and Ignatius, Francis of Assisi and Teresa of Avila, Dorothy Day, John XIII, Vatican II.

A disturbing refrain, however, weaves its way into the more simple song of church history. church authorities often seek power, brutally, and formulate rigid sexual norms as a way of maintaining it. Power is the church's permanent temptation and harsh sexual teaching is the instrument of its implementation. At such moments, compassion is seen as a weakness and diversity, a crime.

One sees this barter of control and cruelty for compassion clearly in the early fourth to the mid fifth century of our era. Notice how a number of issues and decisions, all connected, I would argue, come together in a time frame of little more than a century.

▷ Constantine gives Christianity legal standing, vast political power, and a Roman sense that the law is more important than almost anything else; indeed, law in the Empire is the way power is managed and secured.

▷ Pope Damasus (366–384) changes the tradition of the church and decrees that priests may marry but a sexual life with their wives is absolutely forbidden.

▷ St. Augustine develops a just war theory, actually borrowing from Cicero, which endorses killing as an act of virtue if the motive is not the death of the person; Christians now serve readily in the Roman Army; this theory will later permit the Crusades and Inquisitions.

▷ Pope Damasus in 382 applies Matthew 16, 18, ("You are Peter") to himself and his office, claiming power over every other Christian Community. This is less than seventy years after Constantine's 313 decision. It reverses the traditional teaching until then that Matthew 16, 18 celebrated the faith of Peter as a model for all Christians, not the appointment of Peter to an office with power and jurisdiction. It is difficult to imagine Christ giving primacy to Peter in Matthew 16 when he condemned it for James, John and the Twelve in Mark 10 and 12, as we saw earlier.

▷ A rigid, cruel sexual ethic is now put in place. It leads Origen to castrate himself as an act of devotion to Christ; it prompts Augustine to label "sordid, filthy and horrible a woman's embraces", even in marriage; it convinces him that original sin and all evil is in our genitals; it creates what we would call today sexual hysteria in St. Jerome.

There is a causal connection in all this, I maintain. The passing of a community of equals derived from baptism and one Spirit for all and the rise of primacy and power in the church accounts for this. I do not deny that authority and over–sight are legitimate developments in a community; but the purpose of such authority for the church, as for a family, is the freedom of others from our control. Some Catholics today, even church leaders, take for their model for the church a corporation or a military system in which compliance and submission are imperative. When these become paramount in a family, the family is unhealthy.

I suggest that there is a connection between the church aban-donment of non–violence and its fascination with law, power, and sexual control. This demonic alliance between power and sex makes compassion less and less central. Does not the teaching of Jesus and the example of history show this?

Issues of power and sex tell us also a great deal about the second millennium. The two major ruptures, East and West in the eleventh century and the Reformation in the sixteenth, are fueled by the volatile mixture of dominative power and sexual control. We have not the time to deal with both of these divisions. Since most people know more about the Reformation than about the earlier period, let us discuss East and West. Suffice if to say, in passing, that Luther became the Reformer he did because of the raw power of the papacy, its economic plunder of the churches and its oppressive sexual control of the clergy.

Once again, in a relatively short period of time a number of disturbing issues come together:

▷ The popes seek jurisdiction and control over churches where Constantinople traditionally had been allowed pastoral authority.

▷ Cardinal Humbert, a close friend of pope Gregory VII, slams a Bull of Excommunication on the altar in Sancta Sophia, Constantinople in July of 1054. He rails against a married priesthood and describes in disgust the willingness of such priests to handle the immaculate body of Christ and the filthy bodies of their wives.

▷ Pope Gregory VII in 1075 declares that no one can judge a pope except God, that all Christians must obey the pope, that the church of Rome can never err and that popes are made saints by the merits of St. Peter.

▷ Popes now change the tradition and declare that only popes can call Ecumenical Councils; every council in the first millennium was called by a layperson, one of them by a laywoman, and popes had been present at none of them; papal legates are invited not because the pope is pope but because he is one of the five great Patriarchs.

▷ The Papacy endorses Crusades and the Inquisitions.

▷ Obligatory celibacy for all Latin priests is legislated.

▷ Marriages after divorce are declared concubinage.

▷ Annual confession of sins to a priest is decreed.

▷ Law is used to control the sacraments and marriage so that now, for the first time, all sacraments are declared invalid unless the minister has legal standing granted by the pope; this is the final bitter fruit of the seeds sown by Constantine, the Empire, and their fascination with law.

▷ Innocent IV declares in *AD EXTIRPANDA*, 1252, that torture may be an act of virtue and mercy in the conduct of the Inquisition.

We need not belabor the point. Raw dominative power, violence and rigid sexual control go hand in hand.

It is impossible to imagine Christ demanding obligatory celibacy, recommending torture, or teaching that sacraments do not work, even if need and faith are present, unless the minister has legal standing from the pope. Was it not Christ who assured us that wherever two or three gather in his name he would be present? Where is there mention of legal standing? And even though legal standing can serve a purpose, is the need for it so great that all actions done without it are invalid, always, in every instance? Is love or legal standing the hallmark of the community ?

Could Christ have called a Crusade or conducted an Inquisition? Then, why did we? Did Christ call filthy the sexual love of a husband and wife? Then why did we?

Did Christ do cruel things to people for the sake of institutional order and doctrinal orthodoxy? Then why do we? Did Christ rejoice as he excommunicated the unworthy, declaring the community would be better without them? Then why do we?

Did Christ marginalize women and forbid them to dialogue with him about their status? Then why do we? Would Christ ever have dismissed a Christian from ministry only because the minister married and raised a Christian family? Then why do we?

Our mandate for cruelty comes from our lust for power and our need to punish sexual behavior and pleasure when it does not suit an institutional agenda.

The celibacy Christ wanted most was abstinence from power.

It is a dreadful distortion of the gospel to reserve all priestly ministry in the church and all inclusion in decision making to a group of men who promise to refrain from marriage. Such distortion may lead some to abstain from sexual pleasure and its commitments to gain dominative power over others. This amounts to the barter of one's body for power or personal advantage, a form of prostitution. Clearly many celibates, most celibates, would not do this. But the present church system may tempt many to follow such a course, whether consciously or not.

If Christ could do none of these things, why do we?

Is it not a question worth asking?

THIS TWENTIETH CENTURY CHURCH

There were great moments for institutional Catholicism in this century and we must not be blind to them. They were moments when power and sex were not the issue, moments when we reached the heart of the world and the human family because we were gentle and merciful, compassionate and loving. Nothing else works. Ever. Only this.

The Crusades and Inquisitions eventually came to an end. The Enlightenment had something to do with this as did American democracy.

Nonetheless, as the century began, Pius X sought to destroy not lives as such but intelligence and learning in the church. We became a ghetto against the world, belligerent and supposedly infallible, isolated and angry. Pius created a Catholic Gulag in which all who did not think and speak as one man did would be punished. This was the age of modernism and the penalties were severe: excommunication and denial of sacraments; destruction of careers, reputations, ministries; vilification and refusal of Catholic burial. A reign of terror was created and it sought its victims systematically and relentlessly. The whole world was allegedly wrong and only the infallible pope was reliable. Thus, power, dominative and oppressive, narrow and self–righteous, cruel and sadistic was in place. We had learned nothing, it seemed, from the Galileo trial. It is not our intent to judge the motives of Pius X but we must evaluate the system he created.

With Pius XI, about a third of the way through the century, birth control was condemned as intrinsically evil (Casti Connubii) and Catholic couples were expected to have as many children as Nature allowed. Even rhythm, as it was called, was forbidden. Since Catholics came to believe the pope was the Vicar of Christ and infallible, since no theological dissent was allowed, Catholics accepted the prohibition of artificial birth control as God's teaching and complied fully or considered themselves serious sinners.

Pius XII was considered liberal when he permitted rhythm but only if a confessor gave the couple permission.

And, so, sex was now rigidly defined by an institution which had established dominative power over the church. Masturbation was deemed a serious sin always. God punished each and every sexual act with eternal damnation unless it was between husband and wife whose intent did not exclude the conception of children. There were no exceptions. It was not possible to commit a venial sexual sin. All sexual sins were mortal, lethal, deadly. God responded in anger and hurled sexual sinners into hell without pity.

Vatican II was an effort to get the power and sex issues better focused. The two themes were addressed in a fresh manner by that Council.

The reign of terror conducted by Pius X did not succeed. No reign of terror ever does. Vatican II, in effect even if not by intent, was an attempt to end papal monarchy in the church and to distribute power more broadly. One person or a curial oligarchy would no longer make all the decisions. Vatican II went about this by calling for the following:

▷ Collegiality and the World Synod of Bishops.

▷ A church defined as the People of God.

▷ National and Regional conferences of bishops.

▷ Presbyteral councils and senates of priests.

▷ Pastoral councils of laity and clergy.

▷ Parish councils.

▷ Lay ministries and a vernacular liturgy.

▷ Ecumenism and the Christian autonomy of other churches.

▷ Conscience and Religious freedom.

▷ The priority of Scripture over Magisterium.

The structure to end papal absolutism was set in place and endorsed at the highest levels of ecclesial decision making.

Vatican II was a gentle Council. There were no anathemas and no infallible statements. The church was a great Mystery and it was the community of God's People. Hierarchy was important but it was not primary. The laity could no longer be defined as they were until then, as those who participate in the apostolate of the hierarchy, having no apostolate, mission, or mandate on their own.

All well and good. There was lacking one other crucial item, however. Would the sexual ethic of the church remain rigid and, if not, who would have a voice in its reformation? If this was not settled, power would enter the process again and corrupt the church.

A beginning was made in the Council at the reform of sexual ethics:

▷ Deacons, ordained, could be married.

▷ Married Eastern Catholic priests were honored.

▷ Celibacy was defined as a value but no longer as superior to married life.

▷ The church was seen as a pilgrim people, a journey into Mystery with few absolutes and easy answers.

▷ A review of teaching on birth control was called for; Cardinal Suenens reminded the Council that the church could not afford another Galileo case, this time on a sexual issue.

▷ Marriage was defined not as a sexual contract but as a community of marital life and love

▷ Responsible parenthood required the limitation of births

▷ Marital sexuality need not always intend conception and was fully valid and virtuous as an expression of love and bonding.

For this to be implemented fully and irreversibly, two changes were essential:

▷ The repeal of the teaching that birth control was intrinsi–cally immoral; since birth control was primarily a papal doctrine, this would bring the papacy closer to the church at large.

▷ The end of obligatory celibacy for Latin Rite priests; this too was mainly papal policy; such a reform would give priests freedom and options they had not had for centuries; eventually less uniformity would result on all levels of church life.

Had the Council been allowed to debate these issues it would, I suggest, have accepted birth control as a moral possibility for responsible marital sexuality (as the birth control commissions proved). And it would have permitted the ordination of married men in mission countries where there was a shortage of priests (as the Paul VI letter to Cardinal Villot in 1971 and the 1971 Synod of Bishops showed).

The Council would have put these two troublesome and wrenching decisions behind us and the energy and charisms of the church would have been directed elsewhere.

In an act of power, Paul VI took these two issues out of the hands of the Council, confident the pope was a more reliable guide here than the entire church.

Two years after the Council, in 1967, *Sacerdotalis Celibatus,* and a year later, *Humanae Vitae,* ended papal endorsement of the councilar process. These encyclicals maintain that the papacy could not afford sexual freedom for priests or laity. The trauma inflicted on the church by these two decisions is difficult to exaggerate.

John Paul II became even more harsh, almost obsessed on sexual issues. Abortion, homosexuality, optional celibacy and women get his attention as little else does. John Paul is more restrictive than Paul VI on sharing authority. He has praised collegiality but not allowed it to function; he has gutted the Synod of Bishops, denigrated episcopal conferences and defined the papacy in the code of Canon Law as accountable to God alone. Human rights in the church exist only to the extent the pope permits; Christian unity has fared badly; women at large do not find him their advocate.

We know the story well.

There have been some marvelous moments, nonetheless, with this pope. He leaves the church six marvelous memories which inspire us: his visit to Auschwitz and to Hiroshima; his pilgrimage to the Jewish Synagogue in Rome and to the Lutheran church on the 500th Anniversary of Luther's birth (both of these were firsts for the papacy); his prayer service in Assisi with world religious leaders and his celebration of Gandhi at Gandhi's tomb. The social justice message of John Paul is also admirable.

All of these initiatives, however, come from the pope. There is hardly room for anyone else in such a church.

Nonetheless, the reign of terror of Pius X cannot return. Pius X was preceded by Vatican I's definition of infallibility and Pius IX's heavy–handed policies. There was no endorsement for alternative models of church. John Paul II is preceded by John XXIII and

Vatican II. We all know that there is another way to go about church. The alternative model, furthermore, is validated by conciliar decrees, profound scholarship, pastoral sensitivity, the vast majority of Catholics and the whole movement of the world and the Spirit calling for participation in decision making. Ecumenism, conscience , and women have played roles since Vatican II which were not imaginable at the beginning of the century.

There can be no turning back; Vatican II has survived an almost thirty year assault on it.

CONCLUSION

Allow me to conclude this reflection with a thought about Mary Magdalene and Jesus of Nazareth.

In a woman, and especially in this woman, power and sexuality are sharply focused and take a very different turn from the male reading of them.

It is more astonishing than we realize that Jesus would be presented in the gospels as appearing first to Magdalene.

Neither she nor any other woman in the gospel vies for power the way James and John did. No woman ever claimed primacy in the church because Magdalene first saw the Risen Christ and confessed him in an even more impressive manifestation of faith than Peter's. No woman in the gospel betrays Christ. No woman theologian or mystic ever called filthy the embraces of a husband and wife.

Magdalene seeks Christ on Easter morning after the power of a religious institution buried him with its laws and oligarchy.

She saw Rome do its worst with him. She is the only person mentioned by all the gospels as having been at the cross until the end. She saw the results of naked power. She saw the agony, heard the cries, watched all hope drain from the face of Christ. She heard the last words, the final gasp, the loss of life.

Could she ever be impressed with power?

Whatever Magdalene's sexual history or marital status, it was for Christ and for her an item of no concern.

Power however, is always busy with sexual definitions and stereotypes. It executes the adulteress and gives divorced and remarried Christians a stone when they ask for bread. It calls birth control intrinsically evil even if it leads to love. It makes celibacy a sexual issue rather than an act of love. It singles out homosexuals as the new witches to burn, the heretics against whom discrimination is an act of virtue, the way torture once was. It is not the heart or the face of the homosexual we are asked to consider but the way they do sex. Augustine was once there with all married people; pope Damasus was there with priests; Pius XI with all who practiced birth control or rhythm.

But it is Easter morning in our meditation. Magdalene seeks Christ at dawn, with the stars still visible, a scene like that described by John XXIII in opening the council.

Jesus appears first to her, to the one who sought no power. She is not described by any sexual label. Easter has everything to do with the end of power, of law and oligarchy, of religious institutions which kill the prophets and of all the sexual definitions that are deemed more important than people.

The whole future of the church, indeed the whole church, for one shining moment rested in the heart of a woman, in her experience, in her hope. No apostolic faith brought any of the Twelve to the tomb.

Jesus tells Mary, in John's account, to find Peter, broken Peter, fallible Peter, weeping Peter, terrified Peter and to bring him a Word of life and forgiveness. In effect, Christ asks Mary to tell Peter that Jesus will still wash his feet and hold him in his arms.

If the papacy is built on Peter, it must include the memory that Peter heard the Easter message, on which all our faith depends, from a woman.

We might imagine Christ saying to Mary what the gospel record of her allows:

"You, Mary, go now to my brothers and sisters and confirm them in faith. Feed my lambs and sheep, my shepherd Peter with the bread and the word of life. Bring him home. Bring him here to the empty tomb. Be the church for him. Be me for him"

Mary alone of all the disciples followed Christ every step of the way. She came to Christ on Easter morning with a faith that may be unequaled in all subsequent Christian history, with a courage so great that she risked her life at the cross and risked being dismissed as a fool at the tomb. The church is always born in such a heart, not in authority or structures or power or sexual conformity. Only such a heart brings Christ to life, back to life, time and time again.

The Easter faith of the church begins when a woman says "yes" to Christ. The "yes" of another woman once gave us Christ for the first time, in birth.

Such a moment!

Who would want power or seek sexual control of others on such a morning, the best of all mornings, when God called a woman by name, near the empty tomb and sent her as a special minister to tell all the world that she had just seen the Easter Christ and nothing else mattered.

MAKING THINGS RIGHT

A Tradition of Reform

DEDICATION

I wish to begin with a story of loss. My mother died on October 21,
1995. It is the greatest loss of my life. I wish to pay tribute to her
beauty and grace tonight by dedicating this talk in her honor. This
is my first public talk after her death.
My sister is here tonight. I celebrate her for having absorbed so
much of my mother's goodness.

JESUS...THE MODEL FOR REFORM

Jesus was a reformer. Of that there can be no doubt. The
reform he called for was so radical that it seemed to exclude
religion itself. Jesus speaks about the Last Judgment in terms
of human sensitivity to the needs of others rather than in terms of
liturgical or religious obligations. The reform emphasized love so
strongly that it relativized all the codes of law and custom.

Jesus insisted that people were more important than the
Sabbath, that forgiveness mattered more than worship, that compassion was the essence of discipleship. The reform was aimed pointed-
ly against the power and pretensions of priests and Pharisees. It was
opposed to all human hierarchy and it established the sovereignty of

God in the equality of all believers. Those who dominated and coerced others were called pagans by Jesus; their behavior excluded them from serving as ministers in the name of Christ. For, ministry in the intentionality of Jesus was service and not dominion.

Jesus, the reformer, died in agony rather than allowing religion as he knew it to go on without protest. It is this crucified reformer who is the model for all genuine reform. Had he been more conventional and obedient, more orthodox and subservient, more compliant and submissive he would not have been crucified. It is as simple and awful as that.

The fragile and terrified community which gathered in his name came to believe against all the odds and evidence that Jesus of Nazareth did not die into nothingness. Indeed, he was the Christ, Son of David, Son of God, Savior. It was an astonishingly and thoroughly breath–taking conclusion to draw from the premise of the cross.

This conviction, now a faith, was celebrated in rituals of spare simplicity: water for baptism; wheat and wine for communion.

This was how it all began.

There can be no genuine reform in the church if we lose sight of this beginning. These four points of cross and Easter, of baptism and communion, are the heart of what it means to be a Christian. Reforms merely intend to keep them central. If these four experiences are not central, there is no Christianity.

REFORM IN THE SPIRIT OF JESUS

THE FIRST MILLENNIUM...PAUL

I would like now to select one saint from each millennium of Christian history, a saint who served as a reformer and who kept the church focused on Christ. I select Paul in the first millennium and Francis in the second. They stand surrogate for all the women and men, celibates and married, martyrs and prophets who gave their lives to preserve the message of Christ from being suffocated by the State and corrupted by the church.

Paul proclaimed Jesus Messiah for the whole world. This most Jewish of all the Christian saints brought Gentiles, and Jews into an equal relationship with one another in Christ. He compelled the church to reject Law as the defining element in religion. He kept the cross and Easter central, those experiences of Christ which were least Jewish and most free from cultural and gender categories.

Paul learned from the cross that Jesus was justified and sanctified without the Law, liberated by his faith or trust in God and not by any sectarian system. Paul gave Christianity a Messiah without Law and a Christ without religion. He made the gospel catholic rather than cultural, universal rather than Jewish.

To the Philippians (3: 8–9), he writes:
I look on everything as so much rubbish if only I can have Christ and share in his life. I no longer try for perfection by my own efforts. I do not seek a perfection built on the Law but a perfection which comes from faith.

To the Galatians (2: 16, 21; 5: 1), he writes:
No one is justified by laws; only faith in Jesus Christ does that...if the Law justified us, then the death of Christ was wasted...Stay always, therefore, in the freedom by which Christ has made us free and do not submit ever again to slavery.

In the post–conciliar period after the Council of Jerusalem, Paul the reformer, was harassed by right–wing traditionalists who visited the churches he founded to lead people back to the Law. The traditionalists even had Peter on their side for awhile. When Peter became a restorationist working with a preconciliar theology, Paul and the church confronted Peter. They made it clear to Peter that he was less than the church and had to obey it.

The future belonged to the reformer Paul as it once belonged to the reformer Jesus. Had the pre–conciliarists prevailed, Christianity would have withered, its house churches open to traditionalists alone, its communion services more and more rare, its women made subservient to men in the prevailing patriarchy, its slaves kept in a hierarchy which allowed them no equality.

Paul shifted the focus of the church from Law to Christ. All future reformers would follow this example.

THE SECOND MILLENNIUM...FRANCIS

A thousand years after Paul, the Catholic church was wealthy and deeply involved in politics; it was a military power and a heavily centralized beauracracy; it used law to define itself in a way that Paul would have seen as a betrayal of Christ.

No one symbolized the imperial grandeur of the church of Rome more tellingly than did Innocent III. And no previous Council was a greater display of the pope's control of the church and of Europe's monarchies than the Fourth Lateran Council he summoned.

Innocent was only 37 years of age when he was elected to the papacy; Francis, at 16, was some twenty years younger at the time. In his youth, Francis, was invested in violence as a soldier and in affluence as the son of a rich cloth merchant.

Francis was 24 when he heard Christ call him to rebuild the church, He, like Paul, was a mystic but he sought reform not through soaring theology but in poverty, humility and simplicity. These were the hallmarks of his life. He lived them so thoroughly that many believe there was no other more like Christ in all Christian history than Francis.

Paul's' call for reform was conceptual and structural in its consequences; Francis' call was spiritual and individual, leading to personal conversion and renewal. The two approaches would be the pattern for all reform of the church. Both are needed and both bring the church back to Christ.

Francis was given to poverty, achieving the inner freedom that comes when possessions are not greedily acquired. Had Innocent III and Lateran IV heard his call, the church would have reflected more clearly the life of Jesus and the preaching of Paul. Instead it became the major financial institution in Europe.

Francis was given to humility, manifesting in his life the joy that comes when power is not addictively sought. Had Innocent and Lateran IV been sensitive to Francis, the church of the Middle Ages might have become a church of dialogue and hospitality.

Francis was given to simplicity, demonstrating in his life the non–violence and peace that follow when all creation is poetically celebrated rather than savagely exploited. Had pope and Council learned from Francis, the church would have put less trust in dogma and clericalism, in politics and canon law.

Three years after Francis heard the call to rebuild the church he came to Innocent III to have the rule of his new community approved. Innocent was the ruler of the Western World when Francis came to him in poverty, humility and simplicity. The meeting of these two men, both of whom claimed to be Christ's disciples, was an encounter between two utterly different conceptions of church.

Innocent believed the Roman System could save the world; Francis believed in Christ. Innocent went on to excommunicate the King of England, to declare Magna Carta null and void, and to encourage crusades. Francis went on to bear in his body the signs of the crucified Christ and to carry in his heart the love of God for all creation.

Today no one is moved by the power and privilege with which Innocent III lived out his calling as a Christian and the ministry of the papacy. Today hardly anyone remains uninspired by the poverty, humility and simplicity of Francis.

The church, in its power structure, ignored Francis but the heart of the church felt his life and continues to grow in grace because of him.

THE ROMAN SYSTEM...ITS ORIGINS

There is nothing in the history of the Catholic church which embodies the Law Paul rejected more fully than the Roman System. It is this system which is most impervious to Francis' effort to rebuild the church of Christ.

I do not equate the Roman System with the role the papacy

plays as a ministry of unity in the church. When the papal office is well used it focuses the church's structural life on unity, harmony, and reconciliation. The Roman System is simply not the same as the ministry of unity.

The System, as we know it now, began during the first millennium. The church of Rome claimed the relics of Peter and Paul; it identified with the Emperor and it assumed his place and titles when the capital of the Empire moved to Constantinople.

Nonetheless, the System was under control as long as two elements were in place:

▷ Eastern Christianity was fully united with Western Christianity

▷ The pope had no control of Ecumenical Councils

These two elements are reciprocal. Eastern Christianity is culturally collegial; it stresses liturgy rather than law as a source of ecclesial unity; it relies on mysticism and the Spirit rather than on structure and jurisdiction, episcopal monarchy and infallibility to build the church. Eastern Orthodoxy has its own problems but the assets we have cited are the treasures the Western church lost when the great schism occurred in the eleventh century.

In the first millennium, the pope could not summon Councils or set their agenda; he had no veto power over them and attended none of them. Papal legates were invited, not because the pope alone could legitimate a Council but because he was one of the five great patriarchs of the church expressing its structural unity: Jerusalem, Antioch, Alexandria, Rome and Constantinople.

There were times in the first millennium when the Roman System claimed priority over other churches but this was often dismissed as Roman rhetoric. The church saw itself as collegial; the pope was an integral part of that process but not its essence. For this reason, pope Victor I was ignored when, in the second century, he tried to impose a single Roman date for Easter and excommunicated all of Asia Minor for not obeying his decree.

When Constantine called the first Council at Nicea, whose task it was to define the divinity of Jesus, he did so on his own authority, without asking advice. He writes to the bishops: "It is my will that all of you assemble without delay". Papal legates were invited but the record does not note their making any contribution during the proceedings. Constantine dominated the Council. He laid down the regulations and decided on the number and names of the bishops, the meeting place, agenda, and steering committee. He published the decrees. The first Council was called by a lay person who was not even in the church officially because he was not yet baptized. All other Councils of the first millennium will be called by laypersons, although in these latter cases, they were baptized Christians.

There were two cases of erring popes whom the whole church rejected during the first millennium. They were brought to the attention of the first Vatican Council in the nineteenth century but the political pressure to define papal infallibility led to their being discounted.

Pope Vigilius in the sixth century was confused about whether Christ was fully human. The Fifth Ecumenical Council in Constantinople clarified this doctrine and rejected the pope as a reliable teacher for the church.

Pope Honorius I was formally condemned as a heretic by the Sixth Ecumenical Council in Constantinople and this condemnation was confirmed by subsequent popes and by the Seventh Ecumenical Council.

The Roman System, therefore, is not fully in place for the first half of Christian history.

The Roman System is brought into place only after the East splits from the West. Three popes in particular help to develop this System rapidly and forcefully.

GREGORY VII

East and West separate in 1054. Within twenty years, a pope who is not balanced by collegial structures comes to the papacy. Gregory VII is elected in 1073. He was a man of passionate faith who had a heart of granite. He was fearless, honest, and cruel: authoritarian, unyielding, and single–minded. It was he who equated obedience to God with obedience to the church and to the pope. This mysticism of obedience will become a key element in enforcing the Roman System during the second millennium. It will be expanded in Trent and Vatican I, two Councils in which the popes will dominate and increase their power at the expense of the church at large. Both these Councils are convened during times of deep trauma for the church, the Reformation and the loss of Papal States. There is an unwillingness at both Councils to rein in the unbridled power of the popes at a time when the church is losing so much.

But we are ahead of our story.

In March of 1075, two years after his election, Gregory laid out his program in twenty seven propositions called the "Papal Dictates" (*Dictatus Papae*) He defined the pope as the Lord of the church and ruler of all Councils, and as Lord of the World and superior to all Emperors. Proposition 19 claimed that the pope could be judged by no one on earth; proposition 22 stated that the Roman church had never erred (this despite the formal condemnations of its errors) and will never err (subsequent popes will approve of torture and slavery; will condemn usury and religious freedom; and will insist that the earth does not move and the separation of church and State is evil); proposition 23 notes that every pope is a saint because he inherits the sanctity of St. Peter (the Renaissance papacy will make this claim incredible).

Consider the "Papal Dictates" and the words of Jesus about seeking no dominion and washing one another's feet. Consider Gregory VII and the words of Paul about putting none of our trust in structures and all of it in Christ. Consider the papacy of the eleventh century and the call of Francis for poverty and freedom, for humility and joy, for simplicity and peace.

INNOCENT III

The second founder of the Roman System is Innocent III. We spoke of Innocent when we dealt with Francis. Had Innocent allowed Francis' sanctity to touch his soul he could have been a very different pope. He might have rescued the church from the papal undertow pulling it into the depths of the Roman System.

Innocent was the first pope to call himself the Vicar of Christ. He was one of the finest legal minds of his age and he used law to keep the church in servitude to Rome. The twelfth century papacy made more legal decisions for the church than all those in the previous eleven centuries. Law had clearly become a defining element of the church and an instrument of power.

I suppose it is inevitable that the lust for power, even done in the name of Christ, justifies the bloodshed, sooner or later, done in the name of God. Innocent was the first pope to use violence on a large scale to suppress religious dissent. He ordered a crusade against the Albigensian heretics of Southern France and approved of the slaughter of every man, woman and child identified with them.

It was Innocent also who began the inquisition process. He entrusted delegates with special powers, independent of episcopal authority, to deal with and report on heretics. The pope claimed jurisdiction over every aspect of the Christian life of each member of the church.

How far the papacy had led the church from Paul's mighty words: "Stay always... free and do not submit again to slavery!" Is it any wonder that a sensitive man like Francis would hear in his soul the imperative to rebuild the church lest it collapse in ruin and darkness?

On the evening of June 16, 1216, just seven months after the conclusion of his greatest triumph, the Fourth Lateran Council, Innocent was found dead in the Cathedral of Perugia, forsaken by all, completely naked, robbed by his own servants.

The papacy of power often ends in a bonfire of vanities. Francis died with the marks of Christ on his heart and hands; the whole world still journeys to Assisi in the hope that Francis might make Christ more vital for us. No one goes to Perguia to see where Innocent died.

BONIFACE VIII

The last pope in our trilogy of founders of the Roman System is Boniface VIII.

Boniface was tall, clean shaven, with strongly marked features. He was, however, pathologically unstable: impulsive, high–handed, contemptuous of others, subject to fearful outbursts of temper, incapable of keeping a friend. He had so many statues made of himself that contemporaries charged him with idolatry. He dressed in imperial insignia on occasion so that he looked like the emperor rather than the pope. He claimed to be both.

Boniface declared the first Holy Year in history in 1300. A million people came to Rome to gain plenary indulgences. Boniface used indulgences as an instrument of power as they would be used later as a source of revenue.

On November 18 in 1302, he issued the notorious *Unam Sanctam* in which he defined that there could be no salvation for anyone on the face of the earth unless that person were subject to the Bishop of Rome. At this point, the papacy began to assume the place of Christ. Boniface had become even more than Christ's Vicar.

These were the three popes: Gregory VIII, Innocent III , Boniface VIII who founded the Roman System. All major reform of the second millennium will seek to dismantle that system.

It is noteworthy that all three popes died in misery. Gregory VII was run out of Rome, with another pope named to succeed him even while he was still alive. "I die in exile", he exclaimed as his life ended.

Innocent III, as we have said, was discovered dead in Perugia after he had been robbed and stripped naked.

Boniface VIII died on October 12, 1303, less than a year after he had issued the pretentious *Unan Scantam*. The papal palace at Anagni was surrounded by a cohort of three hundred calvary and one thousand foot soldiers. During the day–long battle, Boniface dressed up one more time, this time as pope. He sat on the papal throne, cross in hand, hoping to stop his captors from laying hands on the pope to whom they must submit if they wished salvation. They seized him nonetheless. A month later, he died, broken in body and spirit, humiliated, encircled by the many mute statues of himself that he left behind. When Dante wrote his *Divine Comedy* during the lifetime of Boniface VIII, he consigned Boniface to the lower levels of the Inferno.

If we move foreward six centuries, to our own era, to the nineteenth century first Vatican Council, we can deal with a further key element in the construction of the Roman System.

Pius IX was, in many ways, a man like John Paul II. He was handsome and had a powerful singing voice. He had an engaging, charismatic personality and crowds responded powerfully to his presence. He began the unfortunate modern tendency of having Rome name the world's bishops. He had a very strong marian piety and, indeed, defined Mary's immaculate conception as a dogma of faith. He canonized enormous numbers of saints and he focused the attention of the church on himself and on the papal office.

He condemned the modern age in the *Syllabus of Errors*. He was convinced the papacy and its infallibility were more important than any Council or the entire body of bishops or even the whole church. In the beginning of his papacy, Pius made liberal statements about the world the Vatican did not control but he refused to allow the Papal States to become a constitutional government.

There were strong reactions to his authoritarianism. His prime minister was murdered on November 15, 1848 and Pius had to flee Rome, in disguise, to save his own life. He returned with a vengeance, sending the papal army to fight the Italian unification forces with a tragic loss of life on both sides. Pius' army was soundly defeated in September of 1860 and he called on the French to surround Rome and protect him. They did so for ten years until the Franco–Prussian War required their recall to France. When the bishops came to Vatican I, they had to pass through the French soldiers guarding Rome and to live in a city under siege.

All of this made the world sympathetic to Pius and he played the role of being a papal martyr strongly to his advantage. On July 18, 1870, Vatican I gave the pope a primacy of jurisdiction over every Catholic community and diocese and it declared the pope's doctrinal definitions infallible even if the majority of bishops disagreed.

When one of the cardinals begged Pius not to go against

church tradition by insisting he could define an infallible doctrine without the support of the vast majority of bishops, Pius contemptuously remarked:" *Tradizione! La tradizione son' io*". *(*"Tradition! I am tradition")

This papacy also ended in misery. On September 20, 1870, the French armies withdrew and the Italian forces seized Rome, some two months after the papal infallibility definition Pius wanted so much.

The Italian leaders promised the pope personal safety, the creation of a Vatican City State, and monetary compensation for the loss of the Papal States. Pius responded by excommunicating the entire Italian government and declaring himself a prisoner of the Vatican.

Near the end of his life, Pius lamented:

I can see that everything has changed; my system and my policies have had their day but I am too old to change; that will be the task of my successor.

During Pius' funeral on July 13, 1881, a group of nationalists almost succeeded in seizing his casket and tossing it into the Tiber River.

Papal infallibility did not stop history from advancing. The Papal States and Rome were taken from the pope; democracies and constitutions, human rights and free intellectual inquiry went foreward despite papal protestations. The Vatican lost its ability effectively to censor books, prohibit dialogue, and control the media. The modern age noted Pius' condemnation of it with a backward glance as it went on to a future of its own choosing.

When Galileo was forced to retract his statement that the earth moved around the sun, he consoled himself with the words: *Eppur si muove*. One might translate: "The earth moves with little regard for our insisting it does not." And so it was and is. The world and the church move on and all efforts to cling to the past are futile.

THE ROMAN SYSTEM...ITS CHARACTERISTICS

It is now possible to define the Roman System. I suggest the System is built on seven key points. Changing any one of them destabilizes the others. This is why promoters of the Roman System resist change so fiercely. Just as Pius IX could not imagine a papacy without the Papal States, defenders of the status quo cannot imagine a church without the Roman System. I find in this a lack of imagination and a deficiency of faith. I believe, furthermore that not having control of the church terrifies those who lose their identities whenever they deal with something or someone they cannot dominate. Just such a mind set once found Jesus of Nazareth a threat and a menace.

Resistance to each of the elements we shall enumerate constitutes the modern reform movement in the church. This movement goes foreward either by a direct critique of the power structure or by a renewal of one's own heart and spirit.

▷ The Roman System is Centralized.

Collegiality on every level of church life is resisted by the Roman System. As we shall see, the two most dangerous Councils in church history are the Councils which called for collegial structures (Constance and Vatican II).

▷ The Roman System is Legalistic.

In the oppressive twelfth century, Bernard of Clairvaux, the great mystic,rebuked pope Eugene III: "Here you have not followed Peter but Constantine".This is the essence of legalism, a reliance on church law to accomplish salvation, preserve the church, and impart holiness. The law thus becomes more important than the life of the church (e.g. mandatory celibacy over Eucharist), the *sensus fidelium,* the participation and freedom of God's People.

▷ The Roman System is Clericalized.

The System requires a mysticism of obedience, one which

necessitates that the cleric be totally defined by the System and allowed no life outside it. Submission of will and behavior, even the assent of one's intellect, is essential. Loyalty and docility are paramount virtues.

▷ The Roman System is Celibate.

The rise of the papacy as a monarchy begins at exactly that point when mandatory celibacy is insisted on and put in place. It is not only celibacy but all sexual life which must be controlled for the System to work.

▷ The Roman System is Male.

The heavy investment of women over the centuries in the priority of relationships makes women an object of intense fear. Relationality makes control and subservience more difficult. This is why all appeals to Christ over church are seen as subversive, naive, or destructive of good order. Women threaten all authoritarian systems: the military, the corporation, the church. This is not to romanticize the role of women who, after all, are also limited and flawed. It is, however, to observe that women working as equals with men keep the System from being single minded. It is not the decision of priests to resign which disturbs Rome as much as their decision to marry women.

▷ The Roman system is Belligerent and Dogmatic.

The Crusades and the Inquisitions are no longer possible. In their place, the System uses psychological torture. Some examples come to mind:

> theologians harassed and put on trial
> the deposition of bishops
> the painful experience of annulments and dispensations from celibacy
> interrogatories before bishops are appointed inquiring

about their total agreement with Rome on all issues

> the denial of communion, for life, for the divorced and remarried

> the removal of people married to or associated with categories of people Rome does not favor, from all employment in church institutions

> the engendering of a climate of intimidation in the church

> the break–down of trust between pope and bishops, between bishops and priests, between pastors and people

> the encouragement by Rome of secret reports on all church leaders in an effort to control all divergent thinking

▷ The Roman System is Infallible.

It admits no errors; it asks no forgiveness; it engages in oaths and distortions to maintain a facade that it has never been mistaken. The infallibility once attributed to God's Spirit is now transferred to the pope; the collegial confidence in faith once attributed to all God's People is now encapsulated in a single papal monarch. The pope then emerges as more than the church, able to judge everyone and to be judged by no one, capable of making all laws and subject to none of them, competent to speak infallibly on his own initiative. This climate is not healthy for the pope or for the church.

THE ROMAN SYSTEM...ITS CONSEQUENCES

The result of this System has been the loss of Peter as the minister of unity for the whole church. The papacy has split the church twice, first between East and West in the eleventh century and, then, between Rome and the Reformers in the sixteenth century. These are the deepest wounds the church has suffered in its entire life. Both were self-inflicted And both happened because the papacy which once strengthened the church and brought it peace sought to dominate the church and make it in its own image.

The departure of the East and of the Reformers, their insights and theology, their life and spirituality has been an incalculable loss for the Catholic community.

Was the East so wrong when it insisted on a collegial structure for the church? Was the East misguided when it saw liturgy as more capable than the law of unifying the church?

Was the East mistaken when it affirmed the compatibility of marriage and ordination? Did the East lose the message of Christ when if offered full church communion to the divorced and remarried?

Was Luther not trustworthy when he warned in the sixteenth century that the Papal States were a danger to the spiritual mission of the papacy? Did Luther deserve excommunication because he called for a liturgy in the language of the people and insisted that the laity be given both bread and wine at the Eucharist? Was Luther an evil influence when he asked that all papal decisions and conciliar definitions be normed by Scripture? Did he dishonor the sacraments when he claimed that they had no meaning unless they were received in faith? Was Luther a bad priest because he begged the pope to sell indulgences no more and to liberate all souls from Purgatory, if he had such power, out of love, without waiting for the right price?

Was Luther not our brother when he proclaimed the priesthood of all believers?

Was Luther not reliable when he asked that papal power be limited for the relief of God's People and for the sanctification of the pope himself? Did Luther lead us astray when he asked that Christian communities choose their pastors and bishops? Did Luther fail to touch our hearts when he asked for joyous singing at liturgy and heart-felt preaching and congregational participation and a central place for the Scripture as God's Word?

From the election of Gregory VII in 1073 to the Ninety-Five Theses at Wittenburg in 1517, four hundred and forty four years had passed. What was the fruit of the Roman System during these four centuries:

▷ the split between East and West became permanent and bitter

▷ the popes gave up all pastoral care of their Diocese of Rome and lived in Avignon, France, for more than seventy years

▷ there were three papacies, one at Rome, another in France, a third in Pisa, each with its own curia, college of cardinals, and papal taxation system

▷ the Renaissance papacy, the most corrupt in church history, followed from1471–1521; it lasted about a half century and involved the papacy in murder and torture, in theft and sexual perversion

▷ there were crusades and inquisitions and more Christians were burned at the stake under the papacy than all the Christians martyred by all the Roman Emperors before them.

Jesus once observed that by its fruits we would know if a tree is good. Was the Roman System a good tree? Was it a tree of life?

Had you and I been alive and known all this in the sixteenth century would we have endorsed the Roman System or Luther?

In spite of all Luther's shortcomings, could those failures of Luther ever outweigh the evils brought in by the Roman System? If we are reformers now it is not because we love the church less or because we prefer to be in dissent. Something deep in us cries out that in the name of God all this must end. Fear and force are not the signs of Christ's Presence or of love or of God's Spirit.

Luther declared on April 18, 1521:

I am bound by the Scriptures... and...my conscience is captive to the Word of God. I cannot and will not retract anything since it is neither safe nor right to go against conscience. God help me. Amen.

Had we heard this then would we have supported Luther or the Roman System?

Today that choice is not necessary because we can see clearly the difference between the Roman System and the church of Christ and because almost all of Luther's teaching became doctrine in Vatican II.

THE CHURCH AS CONCILLIAR ASSEMBLY

Constance and Vatican II were major Councils of healing in church history. Both affirmed the papacy but sought to surround it with a real role for the life of the church.

Our two great reforming saints are Paul and Francis. Our two great reforming Councils are Constance and Vatican II. These experiences, on the highest level of church life, saints and Councils, balance the papacy so that the life of the church is not crushed.

Constance was a four–year Council (1414–1418) lasting about the same amount of time as Vatican II. It was the only Council held in Germany. Constance was summoned because of the emergency caused by so many claimants to the papacy. For thirty eight years, from 1378–1414 there had been two and, toward the end of that period, three popes.

Limits on the absolute rule of the popes were talked about as early as the twelfth century. Gratian, the codifier of church law, spoke of popes losing their faith and of the need for the church to protect itself against this. Jean Gerson, a leading influence in organizing the Council of Constance, observed that Christ asked Peter "to feed my sheep", not to run them off a cliff. In a strong speech before the Council on March 23, 1415, he said:

The final norm, set by the Holy Spirit and transmitted by Christ is the church or general Council...every one, the pope included, must listen to the Council and obey...the pope is not above all law...

Two weeks later the Ecumenical Council of Constance passed the decree *Haec Sancta* on April 6, 1415. This is a truly revolutionary document, never rejected by any subsequent Council. It reads:

> *...this Council, legitimately assembled by the Holy Spirit...has its authority directly from Christ; everyone...the pope included is bound to obey it in matters of faith, the ending of this schism, and the reformation of the church....*

With this decree passed, the Council then sought the removal of all three popes. John XXIII (yes, John XXIII) who had called the Council was deposed the next month, May 29, 1415. Gregory XII from Rome resigned on July 4, 1415. Benedict XIII of Avignon was dismissed on July 26, 1417.

The Council established the norm that the church is more than the pope and, in an emergency, can remove any pope.

There was one more item of business to conclude before electing a new pope. This was the decree *Frequens*. It was approved on October 9, 1417 after the last pope was removed. It called for an Ecumenical Council to be held automatically every ten years whether the pope wished it or not. This decree passed just about one century before the Reformation began (October 31, 1517). Had it been followed there might not have been a division between Catholics and Protestants.

Frequens failed to work for two reasons:

▷ the popes resisted Councils mightily, especially those they could not control; this makes all the more astonishing the decision of John XXIII to call Vatican II unsolicited and on his own initiative; the resistance of the fifteenth century popes to *Frequens* was staunch; the church at large did not have the heart or the energy for another major confrontation with the pope after all it had been through

▷ there were no models in the secular world of the fifteenth century for democracy, participation and constitutionalism;

people were not skilled as we might be now in managing a collegial church with a Council every ten years; monarchy was the norm and it prevailed also in church affairs

On November 11, 1417, Oddo Colonna was elected to the papacy on the basis of the validity of the Council of Constance and its decrees. He took the name Martin V. The Schism was over and the unity of the structured church was preserved, not by the pope but by a Council.

Constance was careful to affirm the papacy as a vital and valuable institution. It did not so much declare the superiority of Council over pope or pope over Council. It did, however, insist that in emergency situations a Council may rescue the church from the papacy. Council and pope were not to exclude or diminish each other but to function in a relationship that is reciprocally conditioned.

The Council of Trent was a reaction against Constance and it carried the day with its papal monarchy because of the fear generated by the Reformation. Any institution in crisis gravitates to a strong leader.

Constance was summoned by John XXIII, the pope from Pisa, as a Council of Reform and Reunion. Vatican II was convened by John XXIII, the pope from Venice, as a Council of Reform and Reunion. Vatican II called the church back to the themes of the Council of Constance. It is noteworthy that both Councils of Reform, Reunion and Collegiality were called by popes with the same name, although one was later deemed an anti–pope.

Vatican II was richer than Constance or Trent or Vatican I because it assimilated not only collegiality but the Reformation, not only the ancient image of the church as the People of God but the modern insight of religious freedom, not only the venerable tradition of liturgy in the language of the people and the Scripture as the church's norm but the newer doctrines of the goodness of other religions and the truth of the other churches. It found room for not only the biblical model of ministry as service but the contemporary theology of the value of the secular world and the sanctity of marriage.

Vatican II synthesized much of what was creative in the Christian experience of the last five centuries. This is why it will endure against all short–sighted efforts to act as though it did not happen or to consider it an aberration.

It has been a long and graced journey. It had to have been a good journey because it began with Jesus and because it tends toward Christ. We who are here are the heirs of a noble tradition of reform and the catalysts for a new millennium. The church must always be reformed. *Ecclesia semper reformanda*. And we are its present reformers, not because we are worthy but because we have been summoned.

CONCLUSION

We are able to celebrate the papacy and choose it. The pope is ours. The Roman System need not be.

We affirm the strength of the Catholic tradition, its capacity to endure, its sacramental imagination, its impressive social doctrine, its soaring spiritual and mystical theology, its liturgical creativity and its massive inclusiveness. We celebrate its missionary outreach, its healers and prophets, its martyrs and saints, its noble, noble women, its self-sacrificing pastors and its breath-taking ability to change. A church which gave the world John XXIII and Vatican II in the same decade is capable of anything.

Our church has been a church in reform from its first day, from the parables we were taught and the lessons we learned at the cross and on Easter morning.

The Roman System is not a permanent feature of the church. It came late in our history, with no biblical endorsement and no apostolic validation.

John Paul II comments in *Crossing the Threshold of Hope* that Communism failed because of its inner contradictions. The same might be said of the Roman System. The gospel creates in the System an inner contradiction it cannot handle.

And so we have no fear. Nothing can stop the Spirit or reverse the reform or annul Vatican II or ignore John XXIII or bring us back to a medieval model of church. Nothing can do that. No one. Not popes or dark inquisitors, not career minded bishops or fanatical theologians, not terrified right-wing Catholics or foolishly liberal extremists.

We too hear the words spoken to Francis: Rebuild my church. And we hear the words of Luther: My conscience is captive to the Word of God. We are the daughters and sons of brave women and mystic revolutionaries like Teresa of Avila and Catherine of Siena, like Julian of Norwich and Therese of Lisieux.

This is an infallible community, not in its popes but in its people, not in its inability to make mistakes but in its capacity to survive them. This community endures not from its own strength but from the Spirit forever moving through it. We break bread and are brought to wholeness in the Body of Christ from the fragments of our lives. We find the church a broken Body but we encounter Easter healing in its every wound.

Let us hear the words which once gave life to the Petrine ministry: "Peter, do you love me?" "Lord you know that I love you." The papacy is a ministry for love. Let us hear the words which once called us all to service. "If I, your Lord and Master have washed your feet then you must wash one another's feet."

If Jesus could cry out on the cross for forgiveness for the executioners, how can the church, how can we, not forgive those who served the church as an institution too eagerly and exclusively and who often harmed the community of Christ in the very core of its being? It is time to forgive all the popes and all the heretics, all the blind guides and deaf leaders, all the well–meaning obstructionists and the terrified inquisitors. It is also time to forgive ourselves, for our recklessness or our cowardice, for our impatience and our timidity, for our lack of hope and our failures in love.

In spite of all reverses and sinfulness, the gospel is still with us and the reform is still alive.

We bear witness that Jesus is the norm for the church. We bear witness that Christ is more than the Law. We bear witness that Francis' message has not been lost. We are the reformers who know and reverence the substantive tradition and we are the traditionalists who are aware of the venerability of reform. We honor the past and we herald the future and we do this for Christ and for God's People.

We are the reformers who yearn for God and long for Christ,

who find peace in the Scriptures and build a church worthy of our children.

The Spirit might have chosen anyone to be the reformers. At the end of the second millennium, it is ourselves. So be it. We shall serve not because we are worthy but because we have been called.

HUMAN RIGHTS IN THE CHURCH

Human Dignity, Rights and the Church

The dignity of the human person is the foundation for the credibility of religion in the contemporary world. Today, people are less moved by the logic or the beauty of religion than they are by the way people are treated.

There are, of course, perennial issues and questions. We continue to search for answers to the most haunting and elusive of our concerns: the origins of life and its destiny, the meaningfulness of existence, the purpose of suffering, the point of ecstasy, the source of the universe's splendor, the reason for love and death, sacrifice and pity, forgiveness and magnanimity.

Religions become credible not only as they give convincing responses to these challenges but as they foster and defend human rights. In a sense, this most contemporary of our concerns is also very ancient. It is love which remains the most convincing of all certitudes.

The respect and devotion of the human family are reserved for those institutions and individuals who believe in human rights. The sense of awe, which religions engender, must now be focused on the human heart and found in the depths of our humanity and in the human rights which allow it expression.

111

The question of human rights in the church, then, is not a marginal issue. It is at the center of evangelization and church life.

The issue of human rights in the church is complex. We might begin by concentrating on our humanity rather than on the nature of the church. The church exists for the human family, not the reverse.

The credibility of the church's commitment to human rights depends upon four values:

▷ human rights in the world at large

▷ sexual rights in the global community

▷ baptismal rights in the ecclesial community

▷ constitutional rights in church law

In 1948, the United Nations issued one of its most enduring statements, the "Universal Declaration of Human Rights". This document is noteworthy for two reasons. It gives us a sense of how the world thinks about human rights. It adds to civil and political rights, already well articulated in the United States and elsewhere, economic and social rights.

Working with this declaration primarily, it is possible to number twenty basic rights which the human family considers essential to our humanity. The effort to define these rights and make them real is one of the great achievements of the twentieth century. In a sense, the second millennium could not end on a more positive note than the medley of rights composed by the global concert of the world's nations.

Although many of these rights seem, at first sight, self–evident, not a few governments fail to guarantee them and the church denies at least nine of them to its own members. This number is extremely high when one realizes that seven of these rights simply do not apply to the church because it is not a government. The church, therefore, denies to its members nine of the thirteen rights it is able to assure.

LIFE, LIBERTY, PURSUIT OF HAPPINESS

These three rights are cited in the United States Declaration of Independence. They do not strictly apply to the church today.

At times in church history, life and liberty were denied to those who exercised freedom of conscience and expression. The church once sanctioned capital punishment, torture and slavery.

The pursuit of happiness is a nebulous concept. It means that people are not denied the opportunities necessary to lead a human and tranquil life. The twenty rights we enumerate would guarantee the right to pursue happiness.

MARRIAGE AND DIVORCE

This right applies to the church and it is severely restricted by it. The right to a second marriage after divorce is denied; the right to a first marriage is prohibited to all ordained church leaders and pastors.

The Vatican has moved strenuously against the legal right to divorce in countries where its influence had a chance of making a difference.

GENERATION AND NURTURING OF CHILDREN

This right applies to the church and is restricted by it.

The church specifies that some marriages must be childless (so–called brother–sister marriages) or without sexual experience. It specifies that no artificial birth control is allowed even if a pregnancy would imperil the life of the prospective mother. It seeks to have governments deny funding and legal standing for all artificial birth control programs.

The church forbids the discussion of artificial birth control as a moral option at all Catholic institutions. Artificial insemination and *in vitro* fertilization are condemned even when the donors are the married couple exclusively. This condemnation strives to declare these options legally unavailable for all, even people of other religious traditions.

In its favor, we must add that when the church does not disapprove of marriage, it speaks eloquently about its sacredness. It also acts as a conscience for the world on the care of children and it expends impressive resources of its own to protect them.

HEALTHY ENVIRONMENT...EMIGRATION

These rights are clear in their naming. They do not apply to the church. The church does endorse their legal standing in the world at large.

DEATH WITH DIGNITY

No one should be compelled to die inhumanely even if the intentions are good.

Intrusive medical procedures, the withholding of pain prevention or vile surroundings invalidate this right.

This right applies to the church and its record here is exemplary for the most part. Questions might be raised about the prohibition of removing artificial feeding from the permanently comatose and about assisted suicide. These issues are controversial in society at large and no consensus about the right to these options under death with dignity statutes has been achieved.

FREEDOM OF EXPRESSION, INFORMATION AND FREEDOM OF MEDIA

People have the right to express opinions as long as others have the free and equal right to respond. The church often denies this right even to its more responsible, scholarly, and well–intentioned members. There is fear in many Catholic circles of signing petitions for moderate reform and of being publicly identified as sympathetic to such reform.

There would be no academic freedom in Catholic institutions were it not for secular law.

Information and freedom of the media involve access to vital information about the public lives of people and institutions. The media ought to be free to disseminate information as long as its presentation does not violate the humanity of others as defined by the world at large.

The church's record with regard to these rights has been appalling.

CONSCIENCE AND RELIGION

In this eleventh right, "conscience" intends the right of people to belong to no religion; "religion" refers to public expression in an organized system of belief.

The church's record here has improved over the centuries and it is not now against this right.

PEACEFUL ASSEMBLY AND ASSOCIATION

Church law does not respect this right. church property is public property, supported by the voluntary contributions of church members. Yet these members are often prohibited from assembling peacefully to discuss reform in free and respectful dialogue. Some groups are even prohibited from having a canonically correct Eucharistic celebration during their gatherings.

DUE PROCESS AND EQUAL PROTECTION

An independent judicial process is essential. There is little likelihood that one can receive an impartial hearing when the accuser is also the judge. This is the present system in the Catholic church.

Other guarantees in secular law are not given in canon law. These include the right to know and face one's accusers, a public hearing or trial, the right to counsel, and the right to appeal to an independent court.

REPRESENTATIVE GOVERNMENT
WITH EQUAL ACCESS FOR ALL

There is no representative government in the church today although its tradition has been collegial. Christians, furthermore, elected their pastors and bishops during the first millennium.

Equal access means that any member may be a viable candidate for any office. To disqualify people because of their gender or because they exercise the human right to marry is arbitrary and discriminatory.

OWNERSHIP OF PERSONAL PROPERTY

Church policy defends this right in the church and in the world at large.

HUMANE STANDARD OF LIFE
(FOOD, HOUSING, MEDICAL CARE)

This sixteenth right does not apply to the church. The church has spoken bravely, persuasively, and often for this right in the world at large. It has also provided necessities for life to many from its own resources.

EDUCATION

The church has an impressive record of providing education to its people through the centuries. For governments, this requires free schooling through the elementary years.

EMPLOYMENT AND HUMANE WORKING CONDITIONS

The church's record here is mixed and, therefore, it cannot be listed as defending this right. People who lose employment in church institutions have no right of redress.

The church often resists efforts of its employees to organize into unions. Not infrequently it pays less than a fair and competitive wage, even as it expends resources in less worthy endeavors. It does not allow impartial, secular agencies to mediate disputes.

Nonetheless, the church supports workers in the secular order in the achievement of these rights.

SOCIAL SECURITY AND PENSION

This right does not fully apply to the church. Where it does, the church has been fair.

PROTECTION OF THESE RIGHTS IN LAW. EQUALLY APPLIED TO EVERYONE, AND IRREVOCABLE

Canon law makes rights dependent on the pleasure of the pope. There are then no meaningful rights which are equally applied to all and irrevocable.

SUMMARY

Human rights must be exercised responsibly and with proper regard for others. Rights may be denied, if a person freely chooses to deny them for a higher motive. One may, for example, give one's life for the sake of love or choose not to express an opinion which may offend another. Rights, however, must not be denied by another person or institution.

One could indict the church before an international and impartial court for denying at least nine of these rights: marriage and divorce; generation and nurturing of children; freedom of expression; information and freedom of the media; peaceful assembly and association; due process and equal protection of law; representative government with equal access to all offices; employment and humane working conditions; protection of rights in law. The first two of the rights are from nature; the next five are civil rights; the eighth is an economic right and the last a general right.

Seven rights do not apply to church structures: life, liberty; pursuit of happiness; healthy environment; emigration; humane standard of life; social security and pension.

Four rights apply to church structures and are recognized by the church: death with dignity; conscience and religion; ownership of personal property; education.

Church leaders might argue that the church is a voluntary organization and that those who find its policies oppressive can easily go elsewhere. Yet the church should not sanction the violation of human rights simply because there are no complaints or because people can go elsewhere.

No one of these twenty rights, I would argue, is against the gospel or theologically in violation of church Tradition. The strongest objection here from some church leaders would be "equal access to all offices" and the disbarment of women or the married from many offices. One might counter that baptism is a sacrament of equality and establishes this right in the very beginning of one's membership in the church.

The Catholic church is a church of such magnitude and venerability that its witness is crucial to the fostering of human rights in the world at large. A church, assembled in the name of Christ, must not be perceived as denying fundamental rights and justice to its members.

The ancient teaching is still true: "What you do not wish done to yourself, do not do to others."

SEXUAL RIGHTS IN THE GLOBAL COMMUNITY

There are four fundamental sexual rights which the human family recognizes as central to sexual behavior and ethics. There are three documents which help in determining this global consensus:

▷ Declaration Toward a Global Ethic (Parliament of World's Religions, Chicago, 1993)

▷ United Nations International Conference on Population and Development (Cario, 1994)

▷ United Nations Fourth Conference on Women (Beijing, 1995)

RIGHTS OF SEXUAL EXPRESSION

Sexual expression, like speech, is a means by which the self is identified and relationships with others are forged. Like speech, it requires substantial freedom and, like speech, it has its limits and may prove beneficial or offensive to others. Like speech, also, sexual expression is the personal language of the individual communicating. It must not become an enforced recitation dictated by an institution which predetermines and controls the expression. Very often, institutions, which deny freedom of speech also deny freedom of sexual expression.

RIGHT OF CONSENT

The world at large judges as immoral, sexual activity not agreed to by consenting adults. Consenting adults means that both parties are adult in age and mental capacity and that they are married or equal in social and economic independence of each other.

The Beijing document lists sexuality as a human right (97) It notes that reproduction should be "free of discrimination, coercion, and violence" (96 bis). There should be, Cairo adds, "equal relationships between men and women" and "full respect for the physical integrity of the human body" (7.34). Indeed, consent

119

includes the freedom "to decide if, when, and how often" to have children (7.2)

Consent includes a willingness to accept the consequences of sexual behavior. The world at large condemns the refusal of responsibility by either partner for the child conceived. The words "responsibility" and "consequences" are repeated throughout the Cairo (7.41; 7.34) and Beijing documents (97).

It is clear that the world's sexual ethic and its articulation of sexual rights is challenging, specific and mature.

RIGHT OF PRIVACY

The world at large more and more leaves to the privacy of the individual, legal and ethical decisions concerning abortion, artificial birth control, masturbation, consensual adult sex by the unmarried, and same–sex commitments. Clearly, every one of these privacy rights may be vitiated by selfishness. No one of them, however, is seen as intrinsically evil so that no exceptions should be permitted.

Religions help the human family when they warn about sexual self–indulgence at the expense of others. This is very different, however, from denying these rights or condemning them as evil. The Global Ethic Declaration observes that sexuality demands that the partners care "for one another's happiness" and reinforce, through sexuality, their equality and mutual love. "No one has the right to degrade others as mere sex objects, to lead them into or hold them in sexual dependency." The right of privacy seems to have gained ground over the decades of this century because of our increased awareness of the dignity of the individual person and the necessity to safeguard this by a defense of human rights. Sexuality was once seen as subject to public scrutiny and judgment. A measure of this will always be there because sexuality has social consequences of the highest order. Nonetheless, a growing sense of the need for personal freedom, an increased realization that our former sexual ethic may have been disingenuous, and an awareness that law does not regulate private sexual behavior well, all of these, have made the right of privacy a better option for the world at large, than the right of community control.

RIGHT OF FIDELITY

The world expects sexual fidelity and exclusivity from those married or committed to each other. "The social institution of marriage, despite all its cultural and religious variety, is characterized by love, loyalty, and permanence." (Global Ethic).

I suggest that the global sexual ethic is sound. It is pluralistic in its expression and realistic in its intent. It allows for cultural, religious and personal variations. It is not permissive since it punishes offenders by law or shames them by social convention.

The world secular ethic is not perfect but neither is that of the church.

SUMMARY

These four rights represent a more reliable sexual ethic than that of the Catholic church. The church pre–empts sexual expression arbitrarily, I suggest. It permits no right of privacy or conscience, declaring, in effect, that all sexual activity is subject to the public domain or forum. The church recklessly, I believe, condemns as intrinsically evil, abortion, artificial birth control, masturbation, consensual adult sex by the unmarried, and same–sex commitments. There is never an instance when any one of these behaviors is seen as moral; every one of them is mortally sinful, at least objectively, everytime.

The church, however, is admirable in formulating a theology of marital and sexual fidelity.

The church puts severe limits on three of the four sexual rights we have articulated; sexual expression, consent, and privacy.

I would add one other dimension to the global analysis, namely, that committed sexual relationships should be publicly declared. Clandestine relationships easily become exploitive. They are kept secret very often because they are dishonest.

Sexual rights are essential for the preservation and development of the human personality. By sexual rights, I do not mean sexual activity. Thus, it is immoral to prohibit celibacy by law or shame.

Sexual rights abide in the person and not in the governmental or religious body. They must not be restricted for the sake of a system or without due regard for the individual. The ready restriction of rights is an assault, a sexual assault of sorts, on the person. It invades conscience before conscience can be heeded. Its end result is not dialogue or persuasion but subjugation and control.

BAPTISMAL RIGHTS IN THE CHURCH

It would be harmful to suppose that one lost human rights by becoming a Christian.

Baptism adds to human and sexual rights. It gives a Christian the right to the full pastoral and sacramental life of the church, the right to preach and hear the Word of God, to celebrate and receive the sacraments, all the sacraments, and equal access to all offices in the church.

The ecclesial community may, of course, insist upon adequate preparation and training before some offices are assumed and some charisms exercised.

The church at large, however, may not deny the right of the minister or the local community by making marriage or celibacy, sexual orientation or gender a prior condition for service. To do so would violate the human and sexual rights of Christians.

Baptism is, of course, more than the rights it confers but it cannot be less than these.

God became human to make humanity the means by which we are redeemed. The church, therefore, must not use the

Incarnation as an excuse for restricting human rights and humanity so that Christians have fewer rights than others. Yet, Christians around the world find more justice and rights in secular law than they do in canon law. This is a scandal.

Jesus does not take away our human and sexual rights in the gospel, only our power to oppress others and to offer them less than love.

CONSTITUTIONAL RIGHTS IN THE CHURCH

Perhaps, the major problem with Vatican II was its failure to create law and structures for its vision of a reformed church.

The church lacks a Constitution, a Bill of Rights, an independent judicial system.

Canon law should provide for these deficiencies and require the following, all of which is in accord with Tradition and all of which was once church policy:

▷ the convocation of Ecumenical Councils at regular intervals, summoned, on occasion, by laity, independent of papal veto.

▷ the removal from office, through due process, of popes and other church administrators who serve the church badly.

▷ full conciliar voting privileges for laity and clergy.

▷ review of doctrinal and disciplinary decisions made by previous Councils.

▷ meaningful participation by the local community in the selection of its leaders.

Church law might also include options which the spirit of the times and the Spirit of God seem to suggest:

▷ the human, sexual, and baptismal rights named above.

▷ convocation of synods of bishops, laity and priests in control of their own membership, agenda and decisions.

▷ limited terms for all church officers, including the pope.

▷ voting rights for representatives from other Christian churches, especially in the selection of the pope as the special minister of church unity.

▷ full sacramental access to all Christians who accept the creeds and councils in the light of the future church we are creating together.

In all this, there must be a decisive voice for the pope but one not able to negate the overwhelming consensus of God's People gathered in council or synod.

I believe that all this will occur in the first century of the next millennium and that the process to bring it about is already in motion.

There is no reason, I suggest, for despair but every opportunity for hope. The Spirit of Truth never dies and the dreams of God's People cannot be forever denied.

The gospel is clear. The Reign of God is for those who promote the rights of others and defend their humanity, who give a voice to the voiceless and an honored place to the marginalized. The Reign of God is for those who see the crucified Christ in those whose freedoms have been revoked. The Reign of God is for those who hunger and thirst for justice, who heal the stranger, the widow and the orphan, and who liberate all those wrongfully held in bondage. The Reign of God is not for the privileged few but for the multitudes who have no shepherd and who wander in the desert seeking the bread of life. The Reign of God is not for the mighty but for the meek, not for the powerful but for the poor, not for those who make their authority felt but for those who make their service available.

The church is most effectively the church of Christ when it is a sanctuary for human rights, a haven for humanity, and a home for those who labor to create one human family, under God, with liberty and justice for all.

JOSEPH'S SON

....
Was Jesus Married?

The title of this article is "Joseph's Son." I chose that title partly
to distance Jesus from too much an emphasis on his being
"Mary's Son." Traditionally, we have associated Mary with virginity, immaculate conception and assumption; we have celebrated
her as "Mother of God" and "Queen of Heaven." To the extent that
Jesus is "Mary's Son," he is more readily seen as divine and
other–worldly, angelic and ascetic. One moves easily from the virginity of Mary to the celibacy of Jesus, from son of Mary to Son of
God.

But with Joseph, there is a different resonance to Jesus. We
move, in Matthew's genealogy, from the sexual relationship of
Abraham and Sarah to the seed of David and on to Joseph and Jesus.
In Joseph's mind, Mary was guilty of adultery and he had decided to
divorce her. One has the impression that Joseph desired a sexual relationship with Mary and that he was grieved that she had experienced
sex with someone else.

With Joseph, Jesus is not as much the child of a virgin but the
carpenter's son.

None of what I have said about Joseph is a later development.
All of this is in the New Testament.

127

The earliest writings provide intriguing information on the family life of Jesus. Paul says nothing of Mary and seems to know nothing of her virginity or of a miraculous conception. Mark, the first gospel, makes no reference to anything unusual about the biological origins of Jesus. He gives the impression that there were at least seven children born to Mary and Joseph and he names them (6:3). There were five sons: Jesus, James, Joset, Jude, Simon; there are, at least, two sisters. Paul tells us more, namely, that the brothers of Jesus are married and take their wives with them on missionary journeys (I Corinthians 9:5). Mark also adds that Jesus is a "carpenter."

Later Catholic theology will make these brothers of Jesus cousins, without evidence, in an effort to declare Mary a life–long virgin. One wonders what is gained by this. Most people find a completely sexless marriage bizarre when a sexual relationship is possible. It is instructive to realize that this sexless marriage is developed as doctrine in the same period when married priests are being warned by church officials to keep their marriages sexless. We must not miss this constant transferal from doctrine to discipline, from teaching about the virginity of Mary and the celibacy of Jesus to insistence on the same for clerics, monks, hermits, and nuns. In any case, the sexless marriage between Mary and Joseph will be utilized to protect our later Christology and to project on the church a spiritual asceticism which is closer to the philosophy of Plato than it is to the teaching of Jesus.

There is no indication that Mary and Joseph had intended a celibate marriage. It seems to have been God's idea because Joseph is confused and Mary is astonished by the revelation that a sexual relationship will not occur in this marriage.

If it is God's idea that celibacy is an ideal way to live and that only a sexless marriage is fitting for the conception of Jesus, God's behavior through biblical history is unusual and unhelpful.

We learn in the first chapter of Genesis that reproductive sexuality is God's first idea and first commandment to the man and woman made in the divine image and likeness. God apparently did not indicate that the divine image would be lost in a sexual relationship or enhanced in a celibate marriage. Why, then, one wonders, would the divinity of Jesus not be able to survive the sexual love of Mary and Joseph?

In the second chapter of Genesis, there is more. The first time God finds something "not good" in the Bible, it is the celibacy of Adam. I do not say this to denigrate celibacy. I celebrate optional celibacy. Adam's celibacy, however, is not optional and God reasons that this is "not good." It is not good for the man to be alone.

The reproductive sexuality of Genesis 1, "Increase and multiply," is transformed into the psychological sexuality of Genesis 2.

For a woman, a man will leave his father and mother, even a church discipline and prohibition, we might add. The woman is worth this. The husband will cleave to his wife and they will become one flesh and feel no shame. God wants no shame when a man loves a woman. How differently will Augustine write later about the sexual love of husband and wife! Why did we hear him and not Genesis?

Adam's sexual joy is lyrical. The woman is bone of my bone, flesh of my flesh, he says. I will leave everything and everyone for her.

In the remainder of the Hebrew Bible, there is not a single instance of freely chosen life–long celibacy. No patriarch or matriarch, no prophet or king chooses such celibacy as a way of pleasing God. God seems neither to want nor bless this celibacy. It is worth noting that this is the only Bible Jesus will have available to him. It is also helpful to realize that Jesus will quote approvingly from Genesis, not from the first chapter about reproductive sexuality but from the second chapter about psychological and sexual bonding. Jesus is not scandalized or embarrassed by marital love–making the way Origen, Jerome and Augustine will be.

If God and, later, Jesus, wanted us to see sexless marriages and life–long celibacy as an ideal, this is a strange way to prepare us for it.

129

A few Catholic writers try to make a great deal of the celibacy of Jeremiah. The celibacy of Jeremiah, however, is only temporary and is related to punishment. In Jeremiah 16:1–4, the prophet is told not to marry or have children "in this place." God asks this of Jeremiah so that the distortion of celibacy will convince God's People that something is wrong between them and God. This is sexual abstinence presented as a warning of an impending national disaster, not an invitation to a life of spiritual excellence and ideal ministerial service.

As Jesus comes of age, neither he nor Joseph have a single image of life–long celibacy as an ideal from the Hebrew Bible to guide them. It is true that, in some instances, Jesus will depart from the Hebrew Bible. He does so in rejecting violence. But the Hebrew Bible speaks, at least, on occasion, about a time of universal peace. The New Testament gives us clear teaching about the exceptions Jesus makes to the Hebrew Bible. But the New Testament is lacking in any model or any clear teaching of life–long celibacy as an ideal for the Christian community.

If Joseph were to prepare Jesus for a life of celibacy, he had no help from the Scriptures.

It is now time to look at the celibacy of Jesus.

THE CELIBACY OF JESUS

The gospels never state that Jesus claims he is a celibate or the son of a virgin. Nowhere else in the New Testament does anyone say Jesus is a celibate. If life–long celibacy is so important to preserve the uniqueness of Jesus, as official church teaching now insists, why did not at least one New Testament writer or one gospel make a point of this somewhere?

Let us try to recreate the climate or environment in which Jesus came of age by utilizing the Hebrew Bible and the second century Mishnah which collects oral traditions going back to the time of Jesus.

We read in the Mishnah that there are five tasks a father must accomplish for his son:

He must circumcise him, redeem him, instruct him in the Torah, teach him a trade and find a wife for him.

The New Testament shows that Jesus is made the recipient of four of these five benefits:

▷ Circumcision is mentioned in Luke 2:21. Circumcision was associated with fitness for marriage. Philo writes that it facilitated intercourse. Martin Buber calls circumcision the sacrament of the consecration of the body and the sacra—ment of sexual intercourse.

▷ Redemption or Consecration of the First–Born

This is described in Luke 2:22–25. It includes animal sacrifice in remembrance of God's setting Israel free from bondage (Exodus 13:11–15; purification regulations in Leviticus 12:2–8).

▷ Knowledge of the Torah is clear from Luke 2:48–49. Joseph is still alive, of course, during this Temple scene. The Torah, as we know, commands marriage and blesses sexual intercourse.

▷ Instruction in a Trade.

Matthew calls Jesus "the carpenter's son" (13:55). Mark calls Jesus himself " the carpenter" (6:13).

There is one item missing.

In Judaism at the time, a wife was selected for a son soon after puberty. Arrangements were made between both fathers with little consultation with the future spouses. The father of the young man was the principal actor because the wife joined his family. The father of the young man paid the bridal price because the son would have no money of his own.

Luke tells us Jesus obeyed his parents (2:51). How likely is it that Jesus did not marry at that time?

Had Jesus refused to marry and had he declared himself a life–long celibate, a behavior so unusual, so much against all Jewish custom and law, would surely have been recorded somewhere in the New Testament.

The general rule in human affairs is that out of the ordinary behavior is etched in the memory, gets talked about, and transmitted. Ordinary behavior is taken for granted and receives no comment.

THE EVIDENCE

Jesus grew into maturity in a culture which presupposed marriage and supported it. A pious young Jewish man would see marriage as a way of pleasing God.

The Mishnah warns:

> When a bachelor attains the age of 20 and is unmarried, the Holy One says: "Let him perish."

Indeed, the Mishnah counsels that "an unmarried man may not be a teacher of children" (Kiddushin 4,13).

The Mishnah forbids living without a spouse unless one has already married and begotten children.

Had Jesus been a widower it would have been acceptable for him to remain unmarried during his ministry. Not otherwise.

We might give other examples but it seems clear that Jesus is part of a culture which identified holiness with marital sexuality and not with its renunciation. Indeed, marriage was intimately bound up with life's very purpose. It continued the human race and made it as much a community as it is likely to be. It regulated sexual life and safeguarded the vulnerable from sexual predators.

It was only after learning the Torah, taking up a trade and entering marriage that a man was deemed mature and fit, at about the age of thirty, to become a teacher of others.

As Jesus learns the Torah, he finds there that all Israel's great models for behavior and holiness are married people. The greatest patriarch, Abraham, is married, as are all the other patriarchs. The greatest leader of Israel, Moses, its law giver, in a sense, the founder of its religion, is married. David, the greatest king, and Solomon, his son, are married, as are all other kings. The greatest prophet, Isaiah, is married and, almost certainly, all the other prophets.

Abraham did not require sexual renunciation before he could become Israel's great model of faith. Moses could behold the face of God and reach sublime heights of mystical union with God as a married man. The psalms did not come from a celibate nor did the soaring love of God expressed by the prophets.

When we reach the New Testament, Peter, the greatest of the Twelve, is married. We know this only from the most incidental information: the curing of his mother–in–law and the observations of Paul (I Corinthians 9:5) about Peter traveling with his wife. Had these incidental items not found their way into the canon, there would have been Catholic scholars celebrating the celibacy of Peter and, no doubt, attributing Peter's special place among the Twelve to it.

In this light, it is difficult to imagine that all the other apostles were not married. Why would they not be?

The sayings of Jesus about leaving family and even hating it are clearly hyperbole because the New Testament and subsequent Christian history do not endorse a literal interpretation of this teaching. Jesus reminds his hearers of the need to honor father and mother and he reprimands the Pharisees for using legalism to avoid caring for parents when they are old. The author of Ephesians asks husbands and wives to love each other and Paul reminds the Corinthians not to neglect sexual love in marriage for too long a time. Sexual love is presented in Ephesians as the best of symbols for manifesting Christ's love for the church. Where, in all this, is there a summons to sexual renunciation as an ideal?

If Jesus called for celibacy, why would the letters to Timothy and Titus make marriage a necessary precondition for church office or equate the prohibition of marriage with a demonic influence in the church? (I Timothy 4: 1–3)

If all of Jesus' circle were unmarried they would be seen as a danger and a scandal. It is difficult to believe that the people of Jesus' time, or ours, would be comfortable with a large group of unmarried men and young virginal women traveling about Israel day and night and living in close quarters with one another. Paul tells us in I Corinthians 9:5 that Christian missionaries, some twenty years after Jesus, went on the road as couples. This may well be because they did this when Jesus was with them.

The Essenes who are not mentioned in the New Testament are not charged with violations of God's intent that all marry because their celibacy is temporary and, in a number of cases, they are widowed. In any case, Essene spirituality is vastly different from that of Jesus. Jesus does not divide the world sharply into hostile and friendly zones. Nor does he invite his disciples to leave the world and prepare for battle. He is not preoccupied with apocalyptic visions of the end time as a primary focus of his ministry.

Some biblical scholars claim that Jesus did not marry because he was too poor. I find this curious. If Joseph was not too poor to marry might not we assume that Jesus, some fifteen years later, would not be? It is, if course, possible Jesus was too poor to marry but it is highly unlikely. It is strange to exclude a possibility of marriage on this basis alone. Even desperately poor people have managed to marry, not only in the past but also now.

When Pope Paul VI, two years after Vatican II, insisted on mandatory celibacy for priests in the Latin Rite, he wrote in his 1967 encyclical, *Sacerdotalis Celibatus*:

> *Christ remained throughout his whole life in a state of celibacy which signified his total dedication to the service of God and people...(Priests) will be more perfect the more free the sacred minister is from the bonds of flesh and blood* (par. 21).

The number of problems in these two sentences is astonishing. How does the pope know Christ was always celibate? To declare, furthermore, that celibacy is a sign of total dedication implies that marriage is less. Was Peter not totally dedicated to Christ? Would celibacy have been necessary for him to serve God fully? Were Moses and Isaiah less than they might have been because they married? Was Adam in a better state without Eve? After the Fall, God does not ask Adam and Eve to remain celibate. It would seem that marriage does not diminish dedication to God. If it does, why do we call it a symbol of Christ's total love for the church?

To teach, furthermore, that priests are more perfect the more they are removed from flesh and blood is a form of Gnosticism. It seems to go against everything we intend by the doctrine of the Incarnation. It invites the development of a dreadful spirituality, one in which every effort will be made to deny our humanity.

Should we not conclude that God should have become an angelic spirit to lead us rather than a human being? Would the priesthood fare better if it were made up of angels rather than people?

How could the pope send out such a letter to the church at large?

These observations of pope Paul are instructive in other ways. The movement from a celibate Christ to a mandatory law of celibacy for priests should not be missed by the reader.

Church leaders, it seems, are prepared to accept a Jesus who is like us in all ways except sexual experience. For many, it is not unfitting for Jesus to be weary, discouraged, hungry, angry, thirsty, sorrowful. The line is drawn, however, when sexual realities are discussed. The letter to the Hebrews, however, observes that Christ can "sympathize with our weaknesses" because "in every respect" he has been tested or tempted as we have been (4:15–16.) On what basis, do we make exceptions to the clear biblical evidence? Why do we do this? Consider the clarity of Hebrews 2:14–17:

*Since (we) share flesh and blood, he himself shared the
same things…for it is clear he did not come to help angels
but descendants of Abraham. Therefore he had to become
like his brother and sisters in every aspect so that he might
be a merciful and faithful high priest…*

THE SECOND CENTURY

The life–long celibacy of Mary and Christ became the subject of
speculation and then, of certitude beginning in the second century.
The second century brings three massive changes into the growing
Christian community:

▷ The destruction of Jerusalem leads to fewer Jewish
church leaders; such leaders were more disposed to marriage as
a source of holiness and as a part of God's original design for
creation.

▷ Gentile leaders, molded by Greco–Roman culture, tend to
equate spirituality with a denial of all physical pleasure.

▷ The Roman persecutions dispose Christians to equate mar–
tyrdom or its equivalent in sexual renunciation with an
ideal way of serving God; sacrifice is emphasized over
service.

Origen writes, early in this period: "Whoever, after the conjugal act… approaches boldly to receive the Eucharistic bread dishon-
ors and profanes what is holy." (*Ezechiel Selections* 7) It is difficult
to imagine Jesus saying this to the disciples at the Last Supper.

Origen reasons that the dry virginal womb of Mary, not mois-
tened by semen (*Genesis Homilies, 17*), is predicted by Isaiah 53:2
where we read that the suffering servant will grow up "like a root
out of arid ground."

The New Testament tension between egocentric self–will and
the call to love others is transformed during the second to the fifth
centuries into a battle between flesh and spirit. church leaders
equate flesh, especially physical pleasure, with sin, and present spir-

it as the sole source of holiness.

Augustine writes in *The Good of Marriage* (10) that if all human beings were celibate the human race would end sooner and the welcome Reign of God would come more quickly.

Gregory of Nyssa laments that his marriage has robbed him of the possibility of life–long celibacy.

The metaphor of Christ as Bridegroom and the church as Bride, a beautiful image, is now interpreted literally. Christ is truly married to the church so that marriage to a woman is seen as adultery if it is a priest "another Christ," who makes the choice.

Sometimes sexual repression surfaces in lurid ways. Jerome writes the following to a group of young women:

Ever let the Bridegroom sport with you... he will come...and will touch your body and you will arise trembling and cry, "I am lovesick,"...Jesus is jealous. He does not wish your face to be seen by others (Letters 22, 25).

Augustine finds Mary's virginity predicted many centuries before by Ezechiel. Augustine believes Mary was a virgin before, during and after the birth of Jesus. He is preoccupied with the condition of the vagina in the interpretation of virginity. Augustine quotes Ezechiel 44:2 and applies it to Mary's body in a way that says more of Augustine than it does of Ezechiel or Mary:

This gate shall remain shut. It shall not be opened and no man shall pass through it; because the Lord God of Israel has entered it.

In *The City Of God*, Augustine speculates what sex would have been like if there had not been a Fall. He reasons that women would have remained virgins with their hymens intact. He, therefore, conjectures that men would have had orgasms outside the vagina and that gravity would have carried semen to its proper place where conception could occur. Thus all sex would have been virginal and intercourse need not ever have occurred.

This is the time frame when theologians and church leaders insist on the perpetual virginity of Mary and the life–long celibacy of Jesus. It is not a period when thinking about sexuality is healthy, holy or even biblical.In this concluding section, I would like to consider a number of questions.

APPLICATIONS

WAS JESUS MARRIED?

On the basis of the evidence offered, I would say there is a high probability that he was. There is no certainty here of course. There may never be. The evidence for the life–long celibacy of Jesus is non–existent.

IS THIS A POINTLESS QUESTION?

The point about whether Jesus was married would be less significant had the institutional church not made an industry of his assumed celibacy. It did this in two areas of church life. It used the celibacy of Jesus, which was free and a gift if it did exist, to fortify a law of mandatory celibacy and to shame and punish those who deviated from it. Surely Jesus, even a celibate Jesus, would not have wanted this consequence from his celibacy.

I would like to spend a moment considering another unwarranted use of these matters by the institutional church.

The perpetual virginity of Mary and Jesus have been employed to implant deep in the Catholic psyche a fear of sex and shame about it. This fear and shame exist in other churches, religions, and societies, of course, but they takes on a special vehemence in Catholicism. Here, sexless marriages may be promoted and a sexless priesthood is presented as an ideal. Here, masturbation is seen as a grave sin and artificial birth control as a perversion of nature.

There is healthy teaching, however, elsewhere in the Christian Community.

In I Timothy 4:13 we read that the prohibition of marriage is a demonic doctrine. Luther writes: "Next to God's Word there is no more precious treasure than holy matrimony." John Calvin, in his commentary on First Corinthians, writes:

> *"It was later than the apostles that men lit upon the remarkable piece of wisdom that the priests of the Lord are defiled if they have intercourse with their lawful wives. At last it went so far that pope Siricius had no hesitation about calling marriage 'an uncleanness of the flesh in which no one can please God.' What, then, will happen to the unfortunate apostles, who persisted in this impurity until their death?"*

Erasmus, by many accounts the most brilliant thinker in sixteenth century Europe, a Catholic and the son of a priest, argues:

> *Should not marriage be honored above all sacraments because it was the first to be instituted...The other sacraments were established on earth, this one in Paradise...the others were ordained for fallen nature but this one for nature unspoiled...I would like to see permission given to priests and monks to marry...Why refrain from that which God institutes, nature sanctions, reason persuades, divine and human laws approve, the consent of all nations endorses...(**Erasmus of Christendom,** R. H. Bainton, NY, 1969, 49–50).*

In this same period, the Council of Trent teaches what it foresees as permanent Catholic doctrine. It denounces and anathematizes those who call into question the superiority of celibacy to marriage (DS 1810).

WHY IS THE WIFE OF JESUS, IF HE INDEED MARRIED, NOT MENTIONED IN THE NEW TESTAMENT?

The New Testament does not name spouses as a general rule unless they have done something prominent in their own right. We do not know the name of Peter's wife although she is still traveling with him some twenty years after the crucifixion during the last decade or so of Peter's life.

We do not know the names of the wives of the other apostles. The New Testament simply assumes their marriages.

The Hebrew Bible, of course, assumes the same. Further information is only given if significant. We only know the names of Isaiah's children, for example, because their names were titles of their father's sermons. (Isaiah 7 and 8)

Magdalene has been named at times throughout Christian history as having a special relationship with Jesus. The second–century non–canonical gospel of Philip states that Magdalene was the wife of Jesus and Jesus was conceived in the normal manner.

I am merely noting this, not claiming it.

Some intriguing things are said about Magdalene in the canonical gospels. She is the only person named in all four gospels as having been at the cross until the end. Generally, only relatives were allowed near a crucified criminal. She is the only person named in all four gospels as having first come to the tomb on Easter morning. She does so to fulfill the task of the wife or relatives of the deceased person, namely, the anointing of the body.

None of this is conclusive; all of it is instructive.

In Catholic theology, we make much of the fact that Peter's name is always first when the apostles are listed. Magdalene's name is also first in the Synoptic gospels whenever the women disciples are named. (Mk. 15:40–41; Mk. 16:1; Mk. 16:9; Mt. 27:56; Mt. 28:1; Lk. 8:2; Lk. 24:10)

I believe the most beautiful Easter story is the intimate encounter between Jesus and Magdalene in John 20. She recognizes him by the way he says her name.

Jesus asks Mary not to continue to cling to him. The Latin translation of Jerome diminished the force of the Greek text. ` Jerome has Jesus tell Magdalene: "Noli me tangere." ("Do not touch me.") This left the impression that the Risen Christ did not want anyone to touch his spiritual body.

We know that this is incorrect because Jesus, in the same gospel, invites doubting Thomas to touch and handle him.

The Greek text is instructive. The Greek verb is "APTO." This is a much more intensely physical word than the Latin "tangere." The verb means "to fasten," "to cling closely." It was used in Greek to describe fastening a shield. It is used by Paul, in a sexual sense, when he writes about a man not touching a woman (I Corinthians 7:1). The verb need not have that meaning. As in English, "touch" or "hold on to" can denote non-sexual contact. Mark uses the verb in this sense when a woman touches the cloak of Jesus. (Mark 5:27).

The from of the verb in Greek has an ongoing or continuous dimension to it. It is not unfaithful to the text to have Jesus say: "Do not continue holding on to me any longer... But go to my brothers and say to them...."

The Greek is stronger than Jerome's "Do not touch me."

Again we must not make too much of this or reach conclusions beyond the evidence. The Greek verb, however, has the potential of expressing an intense passionate, emotional holding, not necessarily sexual, but clearly denoting a deep intimacy between Jesus and Mary. This closeness may be that of a family member or beloved disciple. In any case, it is more than "Do not touch me." I cannot suggest one definitive interpretation but I think the clinging of Mary to Jesus adds enormously to the beauty of the text. Women felt comfortable anointing his feet or sitting near him as Mary does in the Martha–Mary story.

A Magdalene who clings to the Risen Christ represents the resurrection of all women from the inferior status patriarchy had afforded them. It is sad, indeed, that our iconography never portrays Mary, the wife of Joseph, and Joseph, her husband, in an embrace. Whether they had a sexual relationship or not, did they never embrace? If they did not, was their relationship truly human or marital? If they did, why do we never show this? Indeed, in Catholic churches we keep Mary and Joseph apart, at separate altars. Did Jesus never see his parents embrace or show tenderness to each other?

The text we consider tells us that Magdalene clung to Jesus, possibly the way a shipwrecked survivor clings to shore. Such a beautiful image! The woman who saw all the agony of his dying and who died a thousands times as he died now clings to her Savior, now finds him alive after all her hopes seemed to have been buried. What a pity to reduce this text to the weak and anemic, "Do not touch me." How sad it is that we have no icons or paintings which show Magdalene and Jesus embracing on Easter morning! Magdalene clinging to Jesus represents all of us, overjoyed by the Easter life of Jesus, holding on to someone we love and on whom all our hope rests.

DID JESUS HAVE CHILDREN

We do not know.

We do know that if he did, they were not prominent in the New Testament church.

The New Testament names spouses and children when they are important members of the community in their own right.

Some Catholics and Protestant thinkers have stated that Jesus could not have children without their being half–divine, half–human.

One would think, however, that if Jesus is fully human, then his humanity would generate human children. The humanity of Jesus maintains its own integrity and remains intact in its own right.

WY DO PEOPLE REACT SO STRONGLY AGAINST THE IDEA OR POSSIBILITY OF JESUS BEING MARRIED?

Such a reaction tells us a great deal about people and little if anything about the issue.

I find most disturbing not the fact that Jesus was always celibate but that some see no alternative to this. If Jesus can only be all–holy if he is celibate and if he is defiled if he married, then we have made a devastating evaluation of marriage. It is also disturbing to find something intrinsically healthy and spiritual in a sexless marriage between Mary and Joseph. A marriage may or may not have a sexless component to it. This is very different from affirming that a sexless marriage is superior.

IS THIS QUESTION IMPORTANT FOR THE EMERGENCE OF A MARRIED PRIESTHOOD FOR THE LATIN RITE, LIFE-LONG CATHOLICS IN THE CHURCH?

I think it is.

People do feel a sense of shame about sex in different cultures around the world. This may have something to do with our confusion about menstruation or unintended sexual feelings. Whatever the source, a measure of diffidence is not unhealthy in such a personal, intimate and private experience. In sexual experience people are vulnerable; it is not easy to have one's vulnerability indiscriminately exposed.

In the West, especially, this shame is tied up with guilt, sinfulness, and inferiority. Certainly, none of this is from Jesus.

If many people identify sex with sin and with the darker side of their psyche, and if they identify Jesus with holiness and with all that is best about them, then a married Jesus may redeem sexuality tellingly from its supposed demonic and negative characteristics and make it worthy of God in the eyes of all. Conversely, a Jesus who is presented as shunning all sexual commitments and doing so because they are unworthy may reinforce fears that sex is not good.

The reason why some Catholics are deeply upset by priests who marry may have something to do with their ambivalence about a priesthood identified with holiness wedded to a sexuality identified with sin. A married priest may, in the final analysis, redeem sex from some of the negativity associated with it in the

Catholic community.

And so we have raised the question. Let us make of it what we will.

I am asking the reader to consider the cumulative force of all the evidence assembled and not to focus the entire issue on one or another item. John Henry Newman wrote of a convergence of probabilities in some areas of life. This may be one of them.

Before we reject or accept the possibility or probability of a married Jesus, we must also ask what the evidence offered for the life–long celibacy of Jesus is and whether it is as convincing as we once thought.

I wish to pay special tribute to William Phipps whose writings and interviews with me have guided, enriched, and given shape to this essay.

MARRIED PRIESTS

&

WEDDING SERVICES
A Pastoral and Legal Approach

arried priests sometimes struggle with the question of whether or not it is proper for them to conduct a wedding service. There is no easy answer to this dilemma. Some guidelines and data, however, may help create context in which a married, non-clerical priest may beneficially resolve this problem.

LEGAL CONSIDERATION

In the fifty three States and territories (District of Columbia, Puerto Rico, Virgin Islands) of this country, there is unanimity on only one issue: no marriage may be solemnized without a civil marriage license. There is virtual unanimity on the need to notify civil authorities that the marriage has occurred (usually by returning signed copies of the license). These two issues are concerned with registration and record keeping.

There are two other issues, dealing with the clergyperson who performs the wedding. There is virtual unanimity concerning these matters in the States and territories. The first of these is the easier to address. It requires that the clergy in question follow the rules or customs established by the religious society he or she represents (52 of the 53 State or territories include this provision).

147

We at *CORPUS* have never recommended that any married, non–canonical priest present himself as other than who he is. To give the impression that one is acting as a canonical priest in full standing or that one is acting under canonical authorization of the Roman Catholic church is fraudulent.

Nonetheless, one is a priest and indeed has emergency authorization to celebrate sacraments for people when they are in need, when they request these sacraments and when no canonical priest is available. This emergency authorization is cited throughout the Code of Canon Law It is not limited to the sacraments specifically authorized.

The married, non–canonical priest must make a pastoral decision. Is this couple truly in need? Are they requesting sacraments, not for trivial reasons but out of a deep religious concern for their marriage and their relationship with God? Is there, indeed, no canonical priest who can assist them? If I do not perform this ceremony, what lasting impression do I leave with these people about their worth or about the willingness of the church to assist them when they cry out for help?

It often happens that interviews with the couple reveal them to be in a situation which the present church will not officially declare acceptable but which past church custom often found legitimate.

If the married, non-canonical priest is signing the license as a "Minister of the gospel or as "Minister of the gospel/FCM," It is not difficult to establish the fact that one is acting in accord with the rules or customs of gospel ministry or FCM certification. If one signs the form "Catholic priest"("Roman Catholic Priest"is unacceptable), one might explain one's position as we have just done. In this case, it might be better to add a qualifying description e.g. "Catholic priest/Minister of the gospel".

It may be worth noting that Roman Catholic, canonical priests and pastors of other Christian churches sometimes perform weddings which are not strictly in accord with the legal rules of their church but fall within the broad range of its Tradition.

The second issue, dealing with the institutional connections of the clergyperson who performs the wedding, is more complicated. It requires that this clergyperson be in regular communion with the religious society represented (47 of the 53 States or territories stipulate this in some way)

It is not clear what "in communion"means. The civil government does not wish to define "in communion"very specifically. To do so would raise issues of State interference in religious matters. The State makes no distinction between active, resigned or retired clergy.

If one is performing this wedding as a Catholic priest (but not a Roman Catholic priest), one might define oneself as being in communion with the Catholic Tradition because one was and is ordained in it, because one has been officially listed among its clergy and because one is now acting under emergency authorization and within the broad range of the Tradition.

If one is performing this wedding as a Minister of the gospel, one defines oneself as being in accord with the gospel Tradition. In any case, the State will not challenge the legality of a wedding in which the couple and the one officiating agree that this is a religious service, that the one performing the ceremony is seen by the couple as their minister or pastor, and that the minister in question is doing this for the religious benefit of the couple and at their request.

Nonetheless, the officiating person must be careful for the sake of the couple, not to interpret the law so vaguely and loosely that one"s action cannot be defended, if challenged.

We have indicated a number of options a married priest may utilize in securing legal standing for the ceremony. There are, at least, three choices:

Certification through the Federation of Christian Ministries.

This certification has withstood legal challenge in a number of States and is a clear legal authorization to perform weddings.

Delegation by Catholic or Protestant clergy.

This delegation, given for the pastoral benefit of the couple, permits a married priest to perform a wedding service a canonical priest cannot perform for whatever reason. Protestant clergy may grant a married priest the delegation to perform a wedding when the couple wishes a priest rather than a minister to officiate at the service.

Pastoral Judgment.

Since the wedding is non-canonical, the married priest acts not in the name of the Roman Catholic church as a juridical entity but in virtue of his ordination, his permanent standing as a priest (a status the other Christian churches also recognize), his canonical authorization for emergency cases, and his pastoral judgment to assist a couple religiously,

Options two and three are performed legitimately without FCM certification.

We are neither recommending nor discouraging married priests from performing weddings. We are affirming that if they do so, they must settle four questions on legal grounds as they proceed:

▷ a valid civil license from the couple

▷ notification to civil authorities that the wedding has taken place

▷ a viable explanation of how married priests are in accord with the rules or customs established by the society they represent

▷ a resolution in a manner acceptable to the State of the issue of being "in communion" with the church or Tradition they represent

If one has reached this point, a further question may arise. How does one identity his status in signing the marriage license? There are options here as well:

▷ Minister of the gospel

▷ Ecumenical Catholic

▷ Catholic priest

▷ FCM

▷ Minister of the gospel/FCM

▷ Ecumenical Catholic/FCM

▷ Catholic priest/FCM

PASTORAL MANDATE

The theology of the Catholic church gives the widest latitude of any religious group in determining the legitimacy of a wedding. It teaches that the married couple actually performs the wedding, that they give the Sacrament of Matrimony to each other, that a priest is only a witness at this ceremony and that there are instances when a priest or official witness need not even be present. By "priest," we mean either one ordained as such or any other legitimate authority designated by the official church (i.e. deacon or lay person). A couple may proceed to marry each other without a priest if there is no likelihood that a priest will be present to them and that they must wait thirty days or more before a priest is available.

Canon 1116 reads:

"If the presence of or access to a person who is competent to assist at marriage in accord with norm of law is impossible without serious inconvenience, persons intending to enter a true marriage can validly and licitly contract it before witnesses alone:

▷ *in danger of death*

"in danger of death"does not mean imminent death (in articu-
lo mortis), the Latin reads "in periculo mortis"i.e. death is a
reasonable possibility (i.e. illness or impending surgery)

▷ *outside the danger of death as long as it is prudently foreseen
that such circumstances will continue for a month."*

Serious inconvenience"may be due to distance, lack of means
of communication or lack of transportation.

There is no easy way to determine precisely what "serious
inconvenience" means;

▷ even if the couple who marry each other err in the assumption that someone to preside at their ceremony will not be
present for thirty days or more or even if they themselves,
through their own fault, are in a situation where a priest or
other official is not available to them, they may still make use
of this option.

▷ the canon intends the physical unavailability of a church
official to perform this wedding but it is not limited to this;
the canon also presupposes that the couple would be free to
marry each other validly according to canon law but arguments
could be made that canon law does not exhaust the instances
in which baptized Christians have a right to marry.

▷ church custom, furthermore, allows a couple to proceed
without a priest or official if all is ready for a wedding ("omnia
parata") and a priest is not available to perform it. This is a
pastoral option open to a couple when merely ecclesiastical
laws (i.e. having a priest or official perform the ceremony) are
the problem. It is intended to save the married couple embarrassment, expense, or even danger to their reputation.

There are a fair number of times when couples approach a
married priest under these circumstances. The Code does not
directly authorize married priests as such but all priests to celebrate
sacraments with people in non-ordinary, emergency situations.
CORPUS has endorsed an interpretation of these "emergency"situa-

tions which allows people to be assisted when their pastoral needs are great and when the gospel endorses the care which is given to them.

A priest being present clearly means physically present. The law intends this option for Christians in missionary situations. At a time, however, when people have divorced for good reasons or will not seek an annulment because they refuse to declare they were never married, it may happen that no canonical priest can be present to them as a priest even though he is physically in reach and knows that this couple has the right to marry in terms of the gospel and the church's larger tradition. Sometimes, a couple refuses to make a promise to raise their children Catholic or wants a wedding performed outside a church building so that all guests may attend the ceremony more easily or so that none of them will feel uncomfortable. Canonical priests may refuse to perform such weddings canonically even though they agree the couple has a human and divine right to marry.

In such instances, the couple or canonical priests themselves, may seek out a married priest because no other priest is available to the couple. This becomes urgent when the couple does not wish a civil officer or a Protestant pastor to bless the wedding but wishes a Catholic priest to do this, albeit a married priest and notwithstanding the fact that the wedding is not canonical.

The married priest seeks to stay in line with the church's tradition and to ascertain from the couple declarations of their freedom to marry, their love for each other, and their commitment to the spiritual values of the gospel. It is important. however, that the couple remain the center of the wedding process and that the priest not appear to be the one who legitimizes, controls and authorizes the wedding. The priest is there to celebrate what God has done in creating committed marital love in the heart of a man and a woman.

The couple needs to be informed fully of the official consequences of the ceremony. When a married priest performs this wedding, the service is:

▷ LEGAL

according to the norms explained in the legality section of this paper.

▷ RELIGIOUS

God is called on to witness and bless this union.

▷ CATHOLIC

a Catholic priest, working within the Catholic Tradition, performs the service.

▷ SACRAMENTAL

the couple commit themselves not to a contract, but to a covenant and a graced way of life.

▷ NON-CANONICAL

the couple must know that this wedding will not be registered in a Catholic church or recognized by the official church as a Catholic wedding.

There are consequences following from the non-canonical status of this legal, religious, Catholic, sacramental service. A consequence of some concern for the couple may be a difficulty encountered in the future if children of this marriage are presented for baptism. A canonical priest may refuse to baptize such children. He does not, however, have the right to do so. Canon Law does not make a canonical marriage a necessary precondition for baptism. Indeed, one might argue, divine law makes such a condition immoral. Even according to Canon Law, baptism must not be denied if the following conditions are met:

▷ a reasonable hope that the infant will be brought up as a Catholic (absolute certitude cannot be demanded).

▷ at least one parent or a person who legitimately takes on the role of parent gives consent.

If a priest refuses to baptize the children, the couple may be advised either to seek another priest (suggestions and names may be provided by the married priest) or to ask a canonical priest to witness their marriage vows, perhaps in a rectory office. In this latter instance, their marriage is now a canonical marriage and is declared canonically valid from the day they were legally married by the married priest.

At times, members of the wedding party or guests may have difficulty understanding the legitimacy of a married priest performing this service. Pastoral sensitivity and information are the best resources here. The married priest might explain the fact that he is always a priest, that the couple has the right to marry before God, that someone from the church community should celebrate this event and the love of the couple, that the alternative to a married priest doing this might be a civil ceremony or a Protestant service which the couple does not want..

Although we have attempted to give some guidelines for procedure, we must add that this essay remains within the context of law and seeks to work within that framework. Nonetheless, even in this instance. we are describing situations which are sometimes *intra legem* (or "within the law") and sometimes *praeter legem* (or "beyond the law"). Ultimately, the decision to officiate at a wedding needs to be made in terms of wider considerations:

▷ the pastoral needs of a couple who often have no other resource open to them and who feel rejected by the church and sometimes by God when no Catholic priest will bless their wedding.

▷ the illegitimacy of a legal system which allows little open discussion or alternative formulations and which subjects all law not to the community but to the final judgement of one man.

▷ the imperatives of the gospel and the intentions of Jesus for his disciples seem to require a far more loving, forgiving and compassionate approach to people who are, after all, baptized Christians and who seek a blessing from their own church on their wedding day so that the marriage may begin for them

155

with peace of conscience, joy and the confidence that God loves them.

▷ the married priest is always a priest according to church teaching. This must mean something in the real and pastoral order of things; church law empowers "any" priest to aid people in pastoral emergencies; the situations described in this essay amount often to pastoral emergencies and crises of conscience for the married couple.

At some point in the life and ministry of the married priest, the question of what Jesus would have him do is urgent and decisive. We must not spend so much time on law or make it so normative that the gospel, the spiritual life, the needs of people, the nature of priesthood, and the church's more benign Tradition (which allowed divorce and remarriage for twelve centuries) are subjected to Canon Law for their legitimization. A married priest is a priest. This is simple, clear and uncomplicated. A baptized couple seeking out a married priest to witness and perform their wedding service is asking for something good and profoundly Christian. Do we make a better church and a better world, do we make a marriage more Christian by refusing to attend and bless a couple who turn to us in need when they have nowhere else to go?

HOW DOES ON EXPLAIN ALL THIS TO THE COUPLE?

Every consideration and benefit of doubt should be extended to the couple preparing for marriage. People have a right to marry and this right is not to be denied or restricted for reasons that have little or nothing to do with the intrinsic character of their relationship. People, after all, are not meant to marry so that they might please others., churches, societies and even parents alone do not set the norms. The norms come also from the relationship of the couple, from their mature behavior and from the sincerity and authenticity of their commitment. The priest is not a judge primarily, but a minister. Therefore, the priest accords the couple every latitude while acting in a way which is unmistakably religious and responsible.

A couple rarely seeks out a married priest for such a service unless they ardently wish to be blessed and to feel accepted by God at their wedding. It is cruel to deny them this request for empty or capricious reasons.

The main reasons why most couples seek out a married priest rather than a canonical priest are the following:

▷ one or both parties have been divorced

▷ one or both do not wish, for whatever reason, to make oral promises to raise all their children Roman Catholic.

▷ the couple rejects the policy which prohibits a wedding service in a home, outdoors or in a public building other than a church

▷ the couple has been treated rudely or in an accusatory manner by a canonical priest or other church official; or has a disagreement in conscience with church policy.

These reasons provide the married priest the opportunity to make a pastoral response and inquiry. It enables him to emphasize the sacramentality of their mutual love as opposed to the emphasis often placed on external requirements. Some suggested responses follow:

DIVORCE

If there is a divorce in the history of either party, inquiring about the divorce will help the married priest decide if the civil requirements have been met and whether, pastorally. it has been a responsible decision.

PROMISES

Inquiries about the couple's reluctance to make the oral promises to raise the children Roman Catholic will provide an opportunity for the married priest to speak about the enormous benefit of the religious instruction and education of children, especially when it is a family activity involving all members. This places the emphasis on the welfare of the children rather than on the policy of an institution. Moreover, there is little doubt that parents are going to do what they think is right and what they believe is best for their children whom they will love far more than any institution, church or minister. They will do this whether or not oral promises have been made.

PLACE OF THE WEDDING

When couples request the wedding be held at some location other than a church, they usually have good reasons for doing so. This is particularly true in the case of a mixed "marriage." Such reasons involve consideration for the feelings of participants and guests, convenience, sentimental meaning attached to the place, etc. In discussing these reasons with the couple, the married priest has the opportunity to emphasize the need for sacredness and reverence and to help them discern the appropriateness of their choice.

RUDE TREATMENT

When the couple comes to the married priest because they have been offended or treated poorly by a canonical priest, it is an opportunity for the married priest to reflect Christ's healing ministry and to help the couple move on with their plans without dwelling on the treatment they received. Here again, their marriage and their love matter more than anything else.

DISAGREEMENT IN CONSCIENCE

If a couple seeks out a married priest because they are disillusioned by what they perceive as happening within the "official" church, it is an opportunity for the married priest to help them focus on the sacredness of their marriage and the domestic church that they become as family. Once again, it is an opportunity to act as healer and to help the couple put things into perspective.

In addition to the above pastoral responses, the married priest has an obligation to explain the legal and canonical status of the marriage. The married priest might tell the couple something about his own history and something about what God, priesthood and his own marriage mean to him. He should explain how he is legally empowered to perform this ceremony but he should make it clear that he is not performing this ceremony primarily as a legal official, but as a religious person, indeed as an ordained priest. The married priest might add that he is not a clerk but a minister.

Since the married priest is a Catholic and follows the Catholic ritual for the most part, this ceremony is Catholic, although it is not canonically Roman Catholic or recognized anywhere in the canonical juridical structure of the Catholic church. The married priest might explain that there are two possible liabilities for Catholics in a non-canonical marriage or in the language the couple will more readily understand, in a marriage not recognized by the church.

The first of these is, of course, the non-recognition by the official church. We dealt with this question earlier. The priest should explain that this condition can be remedied in the future if the couple wishes by pronouncing their vows again, in the presence of a canonical priest and even in a rectory office. The marriage is then registered as canonical and as having had canonical effect from the date the married priest performed the ceremony. In the couple's language, the marriage is now fully Catholic.

The second of these liabilities concerns the baptism of children in those instances when a canonical priest refuses to baptize children of parents in a non-canonical marriage. We explained in the previous section of this paper that the canonical priest has no right to refuse for this reason alone and we suggested that the married couple might seek out another canonical priest or a married priest to perform the baptism. If a married priest performs the baptism, he might ask a canonical priest to register the baptism in a Catholic church if the couple so wishes.

The married priest should also assure the couple that, if they are both Christians, they are receiving a sacrament. The married priest does not solemnize a contract between a couple but celebrates a covenant of grace between them. A sacrament is not valid because it is juridically licensed. It is valid if it accomplishes and signifies what Christ intended and what the deepest tradition of the church endorses. A married priest is present to assure the couple that their relationship is profoundly sacramental and that they marry in the presence of Jesus Christ whom they ask to bless their marriage. It is in the name of Jesus Christ that the married priest acts. It is the gospel of Jesus Christ the married priest represents. The married priest is present so that the couple will be assured that far more than law and even their love for each other is at issue in this marriage. This marriage is a sacrament, a covenant of grace, as we have said, a mystery in which Jesus Christ and the God who created the couple sanctify them and bless their love, their life journey and, their faith.

RAIN

GRACE

Thomas Merton and Freedom

t was raining the night Thomas Merton began his essay on "Rain and the Rhinoceros". The rain surrounded the hermitage as quietly and mysteriously, as comprehensively as grace or love can surround the human spirit. Rain seems to have no origin except its own spontaneity, no purpose except its own rhythm, no limit except its own boundary.

A human life gains depth from the experiences it encounters. These experiences may be exotic, extraordinary, like encountering the presence of one's deceased father in a hotel room or praying in ecstasy before Buddhas a few days before one dies. More often, the experiences which bring us depth are simple, familiar, ordinary, like praying at a liturgy in Cuba or standing at a busy corner in Louisville.

The entire sacramental theology of the church is premised on the belief that the ordinary is mysterious, eventually infinite, inevitably divine. Bread and wine and oil and water are at first sight, not extraordinary. Every poet knows, however, what every good theologian affirms, namely that grace is everywhere and that nothing which exists is superficial. Ordinary reality is an oxymoron. Sacramental celebration is an encounter with the deepest dimensions of bread and wine or with the endless possibilities of existence,

163

creation and the material world.

If grace is everywhere, then anything can be sacramental. Or, better, everything is sacramental. On some nights, rain is the sacrament. On this night, it was.

Merton's own records note that he finished the essay on December 20,1964. Four years later, also in December, he will die in Asia and be buried, a week later at Gethsemani. The essay was sent to Holiday magazine where it appeared in May 1965. it was published as the lead article in a collection of Merton's writings *Raids on the Unspeakable* in 1966.

We are dealing with a late work of Merton, coming at a time when his life was reaching synthesis and resolution, at least as far as this was possible for such a turbulent and unpredictable personality.

In any case, Merton, assessing *Raids,* writes to June Yungblut, his Quaker friend, that he feels "happy" about the collection. He believes it to be "more personal, more literary, more contemplative" than his other work. The letter is dated March 6,1968, the calendar year of his death. He lists, in addition to *Raids, Conjectures of a Guilty Bystander, New Seeds of Contemplation,* and *Sign of Jonas.*

The rain reaches the poet in Merton. He begins his essay with references to the ordinary gifts of an apparently unremarkable day. He arrives at the hermitage in the darkness, walking through the cornfields after Vespers, listening to the rain as the aroma of toasted bread and the warmth of a log fire envelop him. Merton evokes the elemental experiences which define our lives: bread and fire, rain and darkness, cornfields and prayer.

There was always a tension in Merton between conformity and confronting. He is prophet-with a vow of obedience. It is the prophet who reaches us most deeply. Merton has a way of belonging which keeps him from being predictable. He is, indeed, a monk but he has crafted for himself the script for playing this role and living out this vocation.

Polarities sometimes are not opposites but another way of reaching our destination. Prophecy and obedience may not be as different as they seem. Merton learned that secularity and monasticism were linked. He saw this most clearly at a street corner in Louisville.

This night it is Eugene Ionesco's play *The Rhinoceros,* which leads him into contemplation. He confronts the work at hand but also himself and all of us. His genius lies in his ability to keep these many dimensions going and to write in clear compelling prose.

The rain is unrelenting, God-like in its persuasiveness and its gentleness, in the relief it brings and the challenges it poses, in its capacity to make us eager for it and reticent at one and the same time. The darkness makes the rain mysterious. The sound is everywhere and yet one sees nothing. Merton tells us he sits absolutely alone, deep in the forest, late at night. Here, he writes, "in this wilderness I have learned how to sleep again." It is a silent night, and the rain intensifies the silence, the way music envelops us in sound as it creates silence in our souls.

On this night Merton will assess the tensions between prophecy and obedience. He will raise questions about grace and collectively, about creativity and compulsion. It is a night of some importance for his spiritual life and ours.

SYSTEMS AND SILENCE

What does Merton see and what moves him to appreciate *The Rhinoceros* so readily? Eugene Ionesco's own analysis of his play is that it indicts those who are always in a rush, who have no time, who have lost the need for solitude and have become prisoners of necessity. Such people are depicted as a herd of rhinoceroses. The play is an attempt to summon people to preserve their individuality, to honor their conscience and to resist the pressure to conform at all costs.

Ionesco's play resonates with themes Merton had affirmed through his entire life. It is a play he might have written and one, therefore, he celebrates and promotes.

Merton comes to the monastery because he is unwilling to live a life of conformity. He is driven by a mystic need to be his own person. He does not wish to be a conformist. This leads him, early on, to reject the conventionalities of French and English culture and later, of academic life. He opposes military service, the rigidities of capitalist societies, and the inexorabilities of secular life. He turns to the Catholic church with a passion as a counter-culture experience and to the monastery as a relief from expectations now become necessities, He does not want to be infected with rhinoceritis.

For a time, for a long time, Catholicism and monastic life rescue him. In the final decade of his life, he begins to feel trapped by the very experiences which kept him from being a prisoner of necessity. There is, therefore, a massive display of non-conformist behaviors, of apparently contradictory choices, and startling decisions. He emerges as hermit on a lecture circuit, a celibate who has not resolved his romantic needs,. a Christian who is mystically bonded to Buddhism, a monk who wishes to live alone, a Cistercian who is deeply involved in social protest, a man in Asia with commitments to return to Gethsemani, and to a secular world he will not relinquish.

There are, of course, continuities in his life which go deeper than this surface restlessness. But one of these continuities is an aversion to conformism. He writes to Robert Lax, his friend, in *A Catch of Anti–Letters*, that settled systems sicken him. Systems are the adversary. He does not want to be a captive whether playing prisoner's base as a child or becoming a prisoner of necessity in later life. He shifts identities and opinions with startling rapidity and, at times, it seems, without even a passing reference to where he was a short while before this. There is a unity beneath these multiple possibilities which keeps his life stable and creative. But the unity eludes him and his friends often and for long periods of time.

Merton comes upon Ionesco's play at mid-point in the final decade of his life. The theater of the absurd is a congenial environment for anti-poets who wander in lands called Lograire, sending cables of misunderstanding to the world at large, fascinated with the improvisations of jazz and the incongruities of modem art.

Merton registers a silent rebellion of the spirit against the fleshy demands of systems. His protest liberates him and all who catch his vision.

Merton's last decade of life was focused on protest against tyrannies in political or monastic circles, against economic or ecclesiastical arrangements which benefit the few at the expense of the many. He finds freedom at various times from all this in Gethsemani, in the hermitage, in Zen and Desert Mystics.

More dangerous than the appearance of the first rhinoceros is the acceptance of this by the many who endorse the drift toward rhinoceritis

It was not the appearance of Nazi officials in Germany and in Europe at large which made the Holocaust possible but the endorsement of their policies by the many. It is not the first ecclesiastical decrees which kill the spirit of a community but the enforcement of them by local leaders and passive believers. Eventually, rationalizations justify the legitimacy of the unjustifiable by those about to become rhinoceroses in Ionesco's play or in fascist political systems or on various levels of church or secular life.

A sign that conformism has driven out conscience and that individuality has been destroyed is the meaningless use of language. Merton deals with this in *The Tower of Babel, Cables to the Ace*, and *Geography of Lograire*. We suffer from the malady of conformity that Ionesco calls "rhinoceritis" when our language makes about as much sense as a series of snorts and bellows.

As Ionesco's play progresses, people speak in platitudes rather than addressing the crisis. Their language, like the speech of politicians or some befuddled church administrators, is an excursion into triviality. Those who speak such a language are always beside the point in their references.

One is reminded, in the Nazi era, of discussions about obedience rather than examining the character and content of the orders. Efficiency, train schedules, and camp management were analyzed but not the extermination and genocide which were the real issue.

One is also struck by those in church circles who encourage people to wish for rather than work for the solution of problems and crises. One may, for example, hear rhinoceros sounds about praying for ministers to serve God's People while supporting policies which assure the shortage. Is not human language lost as some trumpet sounds about marital status and gender even though these issues are peripheral to ministerial identity and performance? Language is used to rationalize a position already declared rather than to clarify and explain in a convincing mariner. Can one hear a rhinoceros summons in angry appeals to terminate all discourse and even thinking on an issue because an infallible authority has been invoked?

What does one do about a herd mentality which waits for a lead rhinoceros to determine the direction one should take? Would not Merton enjoy the humor even as he deplored the crisis?

Merton withdraws from the systems which wither his spirit by silently exempting himself from their influence. In the silence, the toxicity of the herd is purged and the sources of language in his life are refreshed. When Merton writes *Seven Story Mountain, Seeds of Contemplation, Sign of Jonas, Conjectures* and other books he shows us a person who has been cured of rhinoceritis. He writes with elegance and grace, on the point, to the heart of the matter.

THEATER AND HERMITAGE

Eugene Ionesco was born in Rumania in 1912. He grew up in Paris. *Rhinoceros* was performed for the first time in 1958. This marked the period when Merton began to change course, moving from monastic and ecclesial systems which once offered liberation but were now confining.

Ionesco chose the stage for his statement, Merton, the hermitage.

Ionesco directed *The Rhinoceros* against the tyranny of usefulness. The reduction of human value to practicality and economics troubled him. Ionesco wanted a flower to be a flower, existence to be existence,. justified in their own right without reference to utility for their meaning. The play alerts us, therefore, to the grace of gratuity, to the festivity of speech and relationship, to the celebration of life on its own terms

Merton catches the mood of the play exactly by his reflection on rain. Ionesco could not want for a more effective antidote to rhinoceritis than a monk, committed to silence,. attentive to the rain in the early morning darkness of a hermitage.

Merton was consistently aware of the anonymous community we forge with people whose spirit is bonded with ours. Often, we never meet them; sometimes their agenda is adversarial, at least on the surface. Nonetheless we form together the company of those who defend life under siege and we collaborate with them without knowing clearly the identities of those who make common cause with us.

Merton notes in *Conjectures of a Guilty Bystander* that we must not suppose that the truth is smaller than we are. This supposition leads to belligerence as we seek to defend that which might be destroyed if we are not vigilant. We might be provoked to attack other human beings who are, we judge, in error, consciously or not and whose error is a threat to the fragile truth we guard. The Catholic church, Merton writes, tends to assume that it is larger than the truth.

In reality, the truth is larger than we are. Our calling is to serve it rather than defend it. The truth will prevail, in spite of us if need be, and it will set us free.

A life or a church built on the conviction that truth is indestructible releases us from the burden of necessity and brings us a spirit of festivity.

Merton's observations in *Conjectures* prepare the way for *Rain and The Rhinoceros*. Freed from the onerous demands of duty, we turn readily to rain and poetry, to creation and liturgy, to humor and community. Merton does not invite us to a quietism which amounts to a disengagement from responsibility. His life and work hardly move in that direction. He counsels, instead, a peaceful engagement for the sake of others and for the sake of the truth, an engagement necessitating neither violence nor fear.

One may prefer the theater or the hermitage for this engagement but the truth is easily at home in either setting.

One of Merton's greatest contributions was this ability to find truth where it abides. He sought to follow its lead rather than to decide beforehand that there were places where the truth could not be found. He transcended, as truth does, the artificial boundaries lesser spirits devise to contain and preserve it.

The church may just as easily become an arbitrary boundary as may the more obvious false limits imposed by race, ethnicity, or gender. The truth is innocent of constructs devised by fearful and self-serving systems. The truth breaks through these obstacles with pentecostal suddenness and creates a universal language of its own making. Truth knows neither Jew nor Gentile, slave nor free, male nor female. It is simply everywhere, able to emerge anywhere.

This sense of gratuity and tranquillity is at the heart of the gospel. Jesus finds the truth in Samaritans and Jews, in Romans and Greeks, in sinners and children, in executioners and victims in sycamore trees and lost sheep, in the Temple and by the lake, in Scripture and the harvest, in bread and wine, in life and death. Truth has no boundaries nor, perhaps, privileged places. It is always gift, not possession. Like rain, it is simply there as a gracious presence.

The hermitage is the theater of the absurd in another key, challenging reason, logic, and cognition at the boundaries where they limit life with sober necessities and grim practicalities.

Merton finds kinship with Henry David Thoreau whose priorities seem, at first sight, so different from his. Thoreau sat in his cabin, Merton writes, and criticized the railways. " I sit in mine and wonder about a world that has, well, progressed." Where he and Thoreau are united most impressively is in the solitude and in the resistance to collectivity. "Just being in the woods, at night, in the cabin, is something too excellent to be justified or explained! "

Merton is anxious that his monastic life not become self-indulgent. He is even more insistent that contemplation not be seen as exotic but as readily available to all, as is the rain, with the joy and festivity rain brings with it

The absurd into which Ionesco's play and Merton's late poetry drift is not chosen for its own sake. This would neither be helpful nor welcome. The absurd, however, set in a larger context, is faith by another name; it is Easter, shattering all rational categories after the irreversibility of the cross and the necessity of the tomb are overcome.

On the surface, Ionesco and Merton are worlds apart. On a deeper level, theater and hermitage are different ways of serving the truth and preserving people from in authentic living.

PROTEST AND PRAYER

When Berenger, the protagonist in *The Rhinoceros*, cries out: "I just can't get used to life," he speaks on behalf of Thoreau, Ionesco, and Merton. Berenger's problem is not life itself but its enforced, unnecessary and destructive conventionalities.

In *The Rhinoceros*, Berenger preserves his humanity by affirming his individuality. He chooses aloneness over compliance and captivity. He will not end his isolation by finding company in the herd. There, one rhinoceros is not distinguishable from another.

Nor need there be any distinction since all think and act alike. One cannot reason with a rhinoceros or as a rhinoceros.

At the end of the play, Berenger cries out that he will never capitulate and that he will remain as the last human being if need be. There is defiance but also despair at the end, victory, of course, but also melancholy.

It is at this point that Merton would introduce another factor in the equation. He would bring God on stage, not a God who makes protest less urgent, but a God who gives protest a final meaning.

Thoreau and Ionesco, quite rightly, do not want God to trivialize the human dilemma by offering victory on terms which keep one from individuality and integrity.

Merton presents a God who does not make the absurd less painful but who allows a life beyond the absurd and shares that life with us.

God, I believe, is not credible to the contemporary world except in the terms Merton proposes. Otherwise, God becomes part of the absurd, someone who usurps individuality, conscience, and freedom.

In his essay, Merton makes it clear that he too has suffered from the absurd. He proposes no easy solution to its challenge. But one always has the rain. The rain merely rains. It does not adjust to our schedule or agenda. It is not of our making. It does not yield to reason or control. It resists secular and ecclesiastical conformity. It nourishes the seeds of contemplation whose ultimate fruit is neither isolation nor despair.

COMMON CAUSE

Merton finishes "Rain and the Rhinoceros" on December 20, 1964. He goes to the hermitage the next year, August 20, 1965 (actually eight months later). He meets Margaret the next year, March 25, 1966 (actually seven months later). In fifteen months these three events occur. I believe there are connections here and that these events influence his Asian journey and journal.

If rain is festivity and freedom and if system leads to melancholy and servility, then the hermitage is a worthy place for Merton and a good place to listen to the rain

The spirit of Merton was progressively unshackled at Gethsemani as the monastic life led him, through its structures, to tranquillity and creativity. Gethsemani released him from his former addictions and obsessions; it allowed him to grow beyond the secular systems which terrified him and held him captive for a time.

Eventually, however, Gethsemani became an ecclesial system which oppressed him with censors and censures , with the Abbot's inadequacies and Rome's intransigence. Then it was that Zen and the hermitage, rain and the rhinoceros, offered festivity and freedom again. Merton was rescued by these experiences and by love, romantic and erotic, from a subtle but lethal form of rhinoceritis.

Merton was, as we know, a free spirit who, surprisingly, needed structure and protest to keep him creative. Without structure, his creativity turned easily to anarchy and self-destructive tendencies. One sees anarchy in the life he lived before entering the monastery and one catches sight of it again as he is given his own way in the last year. Without protest, his creativity drifted into conformity. One sees this at work in such dreadful books as *Exile Ends in Glory*, *What Are These Wounds?* and *Ascent to Truth*.

No one can speculate where all this might have led him had he returned from Asia.

In any case, Ionesco's play came at a good time in Merton's life. It reaffirmed the value of seeking his own way, It strengthened the conviction that he did not want to end his life as characters did in *The Rhinoceros*, by moving always with the times so that one was always indistinguishable from the collectivity.

"Rain and the Rhinoceros" is a refreshing essay because it shows us Merton at his best. It is light and free, airy and inviting.

It has the unrestrained joy of *Seeds of Contemplation, Sign of Jonas,* the early poetry and the best parts of *Seven Storey Mountain.* In the final years he returns to all that was meaningful in the first years of his conversion but he does so with a new sophistication and a profoundly cosmopolitan mentality.

In the initial years he wanted to bring the world into the monastery because he found joy there and a structure he believed everyone required. In the final years he wants to bring the monastery into the world because he finds in the world a freedom and love all should encounter. He attempts at the end to develop a structure to contain the freedom and love. He dies before he discovers this but he does have some elements in place.

The new structure includes not only the Catholic tradition but the other religions and also the religionless spirituality which fascinated Merton. This structure must go deeper than official teaching and conventional religious formalities. It must reach the essence of each religious tradition, the core always recognized as familiar and admired by mystics and contemplatives from all the religious traditions. Merton was searching for this in *Zen and the Birds of Appetite* and *The Asian Journal.*

The new structure finds place not only for obedience and compliance but also for strenuous and public protest. This protest is especially in order when in the church rhinoceroses are not only multiplying but are being promoted and even presented as models of Christian life. Merton was searching for this in *Contemplation in a World of Action* and in *Conjectures of a Guilty Bystander* where authority, infallibility, dogmatism and canonical legalism are sharply critiqued.

When Merton goes to Asia, it is in freedom, without the awful judgmentalism of *Seven Storey Mountain.* He goes there having called for the church to heed its prophetic voices, and to learn from the other religions. He goes to pray to Buddha and to Christ and to find the face of God through both. He does not have it all together. Perhaps he never would or should, But he loves Catholicism and Zen, the monastery and the world, celibacy and

Margaret, Marxist idealism and democracy, the papacy and an open church. He does not see contradictions here because love does not divide into opposites but creates greater unities. And he loves all the supposedly antagonistic polarities. He dies a holy man. All the contradictions brought him to that point. His holiness reveals to us that we judge too rigidly the means people take to bring them to their end. It is what one is that matters in the final accounting. People sometimes use impeccable means but do not arrive at holiness. To make Merton choose differently is to force him to become not a monk but a rhinoceros.

PAUL

LOSS

A Reflection on Romans 5:1-5

P aul was about 47 years old when he wrote his letter to the Romans.

The Romans were not, of course, the imperial Romans who ruled a vast empire. The Romans, for Paul, were a small community of Christians who felt estranged from their Jewish neighbors. They were themselves Jewish, huddled along a bank of the Tiber River, in an enclave, outside the walls of the city, far from the great palaces of the Roman emperors and the civic buildings of the Roman Forum.

We tend to think of these churches or communities to whom Paul wrote as assemblies of thousands of Christians. There were probably only about 50 to 100 Christians in various house gatherings of the Roman church. They formed base communities, domestic churches, all of whose members knew one another's names and faces. They broke bread together, men as well as women, slave as well as free, Jew as well as Gentile.

It was not an ideal or perfect community. It had its tensions. The Jerusalem Council was finished just about eight years before Paul wrote his letter to the Romans. The Council dealt with an issue which almost tore the world–wide Christian community apart. It pitted Jew against Gentile as both sought an adequate definition of what it meant to be Christian. Unresolved ramifications of that Council were still being felt as Paul began writing to the Romans.

There were those, like Paul, who took the Jerusalem Council in a liberal direction. Paul believed in the Spirit, perhaps, as much as any Christian who has ever lived. He quotes neither the letter of the Law nor of the Council, even though he was trained in a rabbinical tradition.

Paul was a passionate man who once sought the destruction of the Christian community. Some seventeen years before the letter to the Romans, he watched Stephen stoned to death in Jerusalem and held the cloaks of the executioners so that they might hurl their weapons with deadly force and lethal accuracy. He returned their cloaks to the killers, signifying to them his approval as Stephen bled to death.

All that seemed so long ago as Paul, now a great Christian apostle, wrote to the Romans.

There had been a softer side to Paul. Scholars suggest that Paul had once been a married man; some conjecture that his wife and child died in childbirth. There is some evidence that he was a widower as a young man.

Paul's faith in Jesus Christ, whom he never met, made him gentle. It led him to write of love in unforgettable words. I wonder if the face of his young wife were present to him as he wrote: "...if I...have no love, I am nothing...I gain nothing; love is patient; love is kind...it does not brood...There is no limit to love's forbearance, to its trust, its hope, its power to endure. Love never fails."

When Paul wrote to the Romans he could not know what we know now, that he and Peter would die in Rome about ten years after this letter was written. Peter would die as a married man, Paul as a celibate. The Christian community at Rome said nothing about the marital condition of either apostle. It loved both men because they loved Jesus Christ. The community at Rome gloried because it was baptized in the blood of two great apostles, confirmed by their hope and nourished eucharistically by their love.

The Letter to the Romans is one of the most influential books in the New Testament. It is listed first among the epistles. Many centuries later, Martin Luther, a man like Paul in many ways, will read Romans and unleash a Reformation.

Paul had suffered greatly for Christ in the years before he wrote this letter. He had traveled on open, dangerous roads and sailed turbulent seas. He had been imprisoned and beaten, tortured and despised.

In this passage, Paul asks implicit questions about whether all the loss and pain were necessary. He tells us resoundingly that it was all worthwhile. Indeed, he is even ready to take pride in his affliction. He believes that he has been justified by faith and found peace with God, not because of what he accomplished but because of what he has lost and what it has taught him. Had he remained with his first commitments and his life as it was, with its greater securities and the honors which went with it, he would have missed so much. "We have been justified by faith", Paul cries out. Not by an institution. These words will launch a Reformation many centuries later.

"I am a believer", Paul reminds us. I may not have an institution to support my new faith. I left that in Judaism. All I have now is a little community of Christians, a base community. I am not welcome in the Temple any more. Neither the Chief Priest nor the Sanhedrin endorse my ministry. I have to make it on faith alone. I need God even more now that I cannot rely on the institution as much. I am justified, you see, Paul tells us, by faith. And God has brought me peace.

Paul asks the Romans to stake everything on faith and not to trust institutions to save them. God finds a place for those the institution rejects.

If you believe in God, God will save you. Later, Luther will make much of this. He will specify it further. You don't need indulgences, Luther assures people. You don't need annulments and dispensations for God to love you. You don't need papal approval. Even sacraments are less than faith.Luther got this from Paul.

If you believe, you are saved. And you are at peace withGod.

"What did I learn from my losses?" Paul asks. I must know if it was worth it.

I learned, he tells us, to believe, to be justified by faith in God alone. The pain teaches me to sort out the priorities in my life. The suffering reveals to Paul that the institution cannot heal him because it cannot understand him or the path he has taken. He has left Judaism and Phariseeism. He trusts now more desperately in Christ and relies with almost reckless abandon on God's Spirit. Suffering has taught him a great deal. He learns to endure.

Paul now speaks from the core of his heart. All the pain was worth it because it taught him to hope for the right things.

What did pain teach him about hope? Paul says it beautifully. Hope led me to believe not in faith but in love. "The love of God has been poured out; it overwhelmed my heart; and brought the Holy Spirit to me."

Hope leads us, Paul intimates, beyond our agenda to the will of God.

When Paul finished the letter, he rolled up the scroll and gave it to a woman, Phoebe, a deaconess, an ordained minister of the gospel. He asks her to bring it to the Romans. It is a woman who brings Paul to Rome.

Our belief in the Resurrection means that our losses will one day come back to us as gifts, as they did for Paul.

If Jesus thought of his mother as well as God in his dying, then, surely Paul remembered not only Christ but also his wife, his lost child, as he went to his death.

Women and children make it easy for men to believe in love.

As we go forth this morning, let us remember Paul's ringing

words: *"we glory in our pain because pain taught us patience and patience gave us hope."*

We are justified by our faith in God, by that alone, by nothing else. This brings us peace. And God pours love into our believing hearts. In this love we know that God's Spirit will be our companion until we die and will rescue us from all our losses.

The only final, irreplaceable loss, is losing God. For, God saves us and gives us back to one another. If we believe in this, we lose nothing in life. If we do not, we have lost everything. ▨

CROSSES IN THE EARLY DARKNESS
Eight Lenten Reflections

I t is the world's saddest story.
The cross in the early darkness is a gathering place for sorrow. Eventually, life brings us all here.

A strange hope is possible in this assembly.

It is not the hope of an easy Easter or a ready response.

When Easter comes too quickly, it dismisses the pain without healing it.

Perhaps, this is why Easter is doubted by so many.

But the cross seems to be in everyone's lexicon of lament and grief. It is the central syllable we choose to formulate our language of loss. It is the key that fits but does not unlock the door, the core piece of the puzzle we put in place even before the tomb is unsealed.

The strange hope of the cross is not Easter, then. It is a hope that comes from merely having a place to gather when the pain is unspeakable and the sorrow beyond all bearing.

There needs to be a valley of darkness for the world. Sometimes darkness needs darkness for a while. When the light is premature, it does not illuminate or heal. It startles us and we turn away from it in pain.

When Dante at long last beholds God in the *Divine Comedy*, it is only after having borne the darkness of the Inferno and the shadows of Purgatory. God appears as light, a light unendurably brilliant and yet somehow bearable for mortal eyes. This light, Dante tells us, bright beyond all definition, did not blind. Indeed, he observes, to turn from such a light would be blindness. And so he stares, transfixed, unable to look away, unwilling to do so, straining ever more ardently to absorb the light as it suffuses every fiber of his being.

Such light and such commitment to it would not help before the prior darkness is experienced.

The cross is the gathering place for the world's sorrow. It is Christianity's most startling symbol, its special contribution to the religions of the world and to the human family.

The loss of God on the cross calls us to God with a compelling summons. The death of God in the early darkness transcends all facile notions of a God of Providence and a God of the lilies of the field. There are times when the God of All–Caring makes it difficult to believe.

Such a God seems inadequate to the gas chambers and ovens of the Holocaust, to the horrid light and heat of Hiroshima, to the construction of a world where 80% of the human family is compelled to survive on only 20% of its resources.

Sometimes the world's sorrow seems bigger than the God of lilies and sparrows. If this be the only God there is, then we may abandon such an easy God for one more adequate to our pain.

The Christ who dies in anguish gathers all the tormented children of the world, all the lost lives and lost values, all the unused graces and shattered dreams, all the world's wasted efforts.

If the whole cosmos weeps, then there is a place for us when our soul weeps. It is then that we find comfort in the cross, in the silence, in the darkness, in our aversion to the light, in our need to have no immediate answers.

Let us gather, for a moment, in the silence, not yet healed, do not try to heal us yet. Let us only be together. Whether it is a child or a church that is dying, whether it is a friend or a ministry that is dying, let us gather. We can wait as long as we are not alone, at the place where God loses everything. At the cross we seem to be able to endure, not because Easter is believable but because loss is universal and connects us with everyone. We can wait, we choose to wait, we prefer to wait, as long as we are not alone. And as long as we know that it is not only we but God who dies.

COMMUNITY

It is not the achievements of Jesus which make us believers but the losses. The miracles gain our attention but the losses win our hearts. Through them, Jesus reaches for community, relationship and longing.

It is a story endlessly repeated in all our lives.

We wander from our parents as children until the fear of being alone or the pain of falling, bring us back to their arms. We return with an intensity and choice we did not experience earlier.

We compete and prevail as adults until the complexity of our success or the agony of our defeats make us search for someone to hear us and heal us.

Losses impose limits and throw us back on our selves rudely. Confined to the self we grow miserable. Community becomes the path we choose out of the self into the larger domains of relationship and grace.

And so it was with Jesus.

The gospels portray Jesus yearning for community as the losses in his life intensify. He wonders about whether there will be any community of faith left in the future. He grows impatient as the disciples fail to understand and accept him, in large measure because they cannot absorb the notion of a defeated Messiah. Jesus laments the unwillingness of Jerusalem to appreciate how much he cared for it.

At the end, he gathers his friends and asks to be remembered. He breaks bread, calls for companionship in the Garden, and cries on the cross not to be left alone.

It is as though God were not enough for him. We do not mean, of course, that God, in some absolute sense, is not sufficient but that Jesus is profoundly committed to his friends even when the intent is not a religious one. Friendship is never friendship in religious terms; it is friendship in human terms or else it is not friendship.

The longing Jesus speaks of to share a final meal with his disciples is personal and thoroughly human. As the inevitability of a tragic end to his life overwhelms him, he veers between ardent prayers to God and heart–felt petitions to his sleeping disciples.

Our humanity requires both God and people for its development, the divine and the human, the transcendent and the proximate.

The contemporary world offers helpful but incomplete support. It fosters community and relationship but it speaks little of God. The world provides people with massive resources to heal our shattered self–image or our broken bonds with others.

The contemporary world, however, is silent about our soul, our interior life, silent also about the restlessness that no human achievement or person can satisfy. God embarrasses the contemporary world.

That which embarrasses us is often the most important experience to encounter. Avoiding God, nonetheless, is an impossibility or, better, it is a possibility with consequences. These consequences are less satisfying than dealing with God. One can elude love but not without consequences. One can neglect God but not without some essential loss.

The contemporary world helps us as we seek healthy relationships. It is far less adroit when God is the hunger we feel.

The present church, on the other hand, does not tell us sufficiently that the ultimate grace is friendship and that the sin–unto–death is our betrayal of one another. In Dante's Inferno, betrayal is the worst of all evils. It is punished in the pit of Hell. It defines the character and face of Satan. I think Dante had it right.

The church does not put its energy into our relationships. For this reason, it seeks our obedience, rather than our passion, as though it were the God it preaches.

In a sense, the most surprising of all revelations the Incarnation offers, is the need God has for us. What we have called before the insufficiency of God is Jesus' constant message. We do not mean this insufficiency in some metaphysical construct. There may not be a better way to get the idea across than with this imprecise language. The description of the Judgment in Matthew's gospel is focused on how to deal with one another. It condemns not our indifference to God, which remarkably is not even an issue, but our neglect of one another. God is present as the one to whom we are ultimately accountable. But the accounting has to do with the ways we support or fail one another.

The point of all grace and sacrament is relationship with one another. These relationships create the church, build the Reign of God, and make paradise worthwhile.

GRACE

Jesus always saw beneath the surface.

He saw how deep and infinite humanity is, connecting with divinity and flowing into the endless sea of the divine.

He saw more than sight could offer. He saw wine when water failed, an apostle in a fisherman, a saint in an adulterous woman, a missionary in a promiscuous Samaritan. He went to the heart, the core, the essence.

He found forgiveness for executioners and learned to trust as death approached rapidly. On the surface, things appeared desperate and impossible. But Jesus did not dwell there.

To see beneath the surface is to behold a sacramental universe.

Of all the Christian churches, Catholicism may affirm sacraments and celebrate them most frequently, more intensely.

It is time now for the Catholic church to see beneath the surface agnosticism and materialism of the contemporary world. For, I believe, that beneath this surface there is grace, a wordless faith, a speechless hope, an inarticulate love. It is Catholicism which can see this most clearly if it has eyes to see. It is Catholicism which can proclaim this most credibly by giving voice to the unspoken grace of contemporary life.

Were Jesus here, he would see more than the surface flaws and failures of a perennially imperfect world.

Let us go out to the desert and wilderness of the contemporary world. Not to see a reed shaken by the wind of disbelief; not to rail against the soft garments, hard money and palaces of the affluent aristocrats. There is time for this. But there is more. There is more.

It may never have been more difficult in all of human history to raise children than it is now. Yet there are children everywhere. Never before has marriage been more demanding. Yet the contemporary world believes in the capacity of marriage to bring happiness.

People today choose marriage rather than settle for it. They need it to be a relationship rather than a contract, a community rather than an arrangement, a journey into the unknown rather than a predefined structure.

There is grace in all this and a measure of faith and a hope in love. And there is magnanimity and vulnerability, ambiguity and trepidation, sacrifice and daring. Always the wine of goodness is possible beneath the surface water of selfishness and transiency.

One sees this grace surface often in the films and plays of our era. Even in their titles, they speak of mission and fields of dreams, about Babette's feast and Shawshank Redemption. There is, you see, grace everywhere, visible, palpable, not far from the surface, out of sight but not beyond reach.

Henry David Thoreau once observed that he did not wish to end his life without every having known its potential, its promise, its purpose. What a pity it would be if we who lived in such a century saw only its sins and not its substance, numbered all its vices and not its victories, knew all the grief and none of the glory.

Such is not the calling of a Christian.

In the tangled complexity and dispiriting debris of modern life, there is striving to make life better. This is the century when we were outraged by poverty rather than accepting it as the normal course of events. This is the century where we sought to make work meaningful and to express ourselves through it. This is the century when the oppression of women was seen for the evil it is and when human beings were deemed to have irrevocable rights and fundamental freedoms.

We need no one else to name our sins. The woman taken in adultery did not need one more accuser. The Samaritan at the well did not need one more man to tell her she was inadequate. The frightened outcast in the sycamore tree did not need one more person to brand him as dishonest.

A time for grace has come. A time to see the grace, sacramentally hidden beneath the surface of the commonplace and banal, the hostile and the seemingly irredeemable. A time for grace has come. A time to behold the beauty beneath the sometimes ugly surface, the bravery beneath the trembling exterior, the ideals that a life of compromises does not destroy, the survivor who surfaces, against all the odds, defying every prediction of loss and death.

SPIRIT

Where did we ever get the notion that the Spirit settles us?

Scripture gives strong witness in another direction.

Abraham is summoned from his fields and flocks to the open roads where there are no markers and where neither distance nor direction can be readily measured.

Moses is driven into the desert where the security of easier definitions and accessible certitudes becomes elusive. Indeed, nostalgia for the slavery once deemed unbearable reaches those recently set free and leads them to regret their liberation. It will not be the last time a mirage such as this distorts reality.

Liberty is unsettling. Slavery and confinement are predictable, somehow less demanding and costly.

The Spirit urges us into freedom, an experience which at least for a time, is isolating, terrifying, unsettling, downright disturbing. The tranquillity of the Spirit comes after the crucifixion, not before, and in no instance, as a substitute for it. Even Easter is not an event of quiet resolution, for Christ or the disciples.

The Spirit is fire and flame, a restless wind, a turbulent sea, an upsetter, a supplanter, forever choosing Abel over Cain, Issac over Esau, Joseph over the older brothers, a maid of Nazareth to be mother of the Messiah, the prodigal son over the dutiful brother, the Samaritan heretic over Jewish priests and Levites, the widow's mite over the large donations, a lost sheep over ninety–nine safe ones, a woman with an alabaster jar of ointment over the elegant leaders of Jerusalem, a befuddled fisherman to become Peter, an enemy of the church to become the apostle to the Gentiles, Magdalene over the Twelve to announce the Resurrection.

Upsetter! Supplanter! Eye of the Hurricane! Turbulent Twister of Settled Systems! Teacher of Words to Stammering Prophets! Instructor of Languages to Pentecost Preachers!

Where did we ever get the notion that the Spirit settles us?

190

Scripture teaches that a child shall lead us, that the poor are honored, the powerful marginalized, and that the hungry and homeless are sacraments of Christ.

It is not difficult, then, to believe that perhaps no Council of the church after Jerusalem had so clearly about it the presence of the Spirit than Vatican II. It upended everything.

It told us that we could all speak our own languages in liturgy and understand one another nonetheless in its worship, that the world was a sacred place and that the church belonged to God's People, that the Reformers of old were essentially right and that those once called heretics were to be invited to our Eucharistic celebrations and, on occasion, to participate in our sacraments. It told us that married priests were exemplary, that the family was a domestic church, that the baptized were not servants but collaborators with their bishop, that the Bible was the church's surest guide, and that the church must always be reformed. One does not reform that which is perfect or even working as it should.

Vatican II called for religious freedom, the primacy of conscience, community with believers in the world's diverse religions, a collegial government for the church, a pilgrim spirituality, and a global sensitivity to the hopes and joys of the entire human family.

Is it any wonder that we came from the Council blinded by the light, wandering on Damascus roads all over the world, hearing voices we had never heard before, asking that our former enemies receive us, ready now to give our lives to causes we once thought God did not favor?

Creative disorientation is the most credible sign that we are in the presence of the Spirit.

Israel wanted a Messiah to restore its institutional integrity. It got a crucified prophet who changed the rules so drastically that the old order could no longer be maintained. The New Testament Christian Community originally wanted its members to be homogeneously Jewish. It got instead a Gentile population that made the past impossible to continue or restore.

Where did we ever get the notion that the Spirit settles us?

The life of Jesus ends in a jarring series of events that were unpredictable and overwhelming. He transforms the Passover and the cross, the judicial verdict and the establishment's judgment, the rules by which ministry is normed and the very order of things decreed by death and its irreversible consequences.

Spirit of God! Do we know what we pray for when we ask for the Spirit to enter our lives, to guide our church, to lead us into the future? Rebirth is as wild and terrifying as birth. But, oh, to be born! To come into the world hungry and thirsty and naked, struggling free from the prison of our confinement, homeless and weeping. And to find ourselves in the arms of all the Christs of this world who assure us that God is a Mother and that we shall not be lost.

So much disorientation! Supplanted, usurped, breathing the air of freedom for the first time, feeling the grace in our lungs, seeing the darkness pass from shadows to light.

The Spirit forever gives us a new world. And assures us we shall not perish in it.

Why would we return to the womb when a new world beckons and the future emerges at every bend of the open road? It is good to be here. Let us not build tabernacles on the mountain tops to keep us forever stable. Rather let us hasten, transfigured, into the future where all pilgrims are compelled to live by hope.

CONFLICT

Why does it not get better?

Should peace be so unattainable? With so much intelligence, with so many who claim that peace is their intent, should peace be so impossible?

Why does it not get better?

One would have supposed that, by now, the world's religions would have brought peace to the global community. Granted what they preach, granted the multitudes who hear their voice, one would have expected more.

Why does it not get better?

If we abandon religion for civic life, there is scarce improvement. Ministers of State do not rescue us any more than ministers of God did. Salvation in the name of a secular system is not more inviting than salvation in the name of a distant deity.

There are, of course, better moments in all systems. Religions summon us to compelling ideals. Society builds structure of support in the acute moments of life.

But there has never been a time of peace when all the weapons are gone and the killing stops, when all the wounds are healed and the pain ceases.

Instead we have memories that torment us, the magnitude of our failure: the bunkers of Berlin and the bombs in Bosnia, the trenches of Verdun and the jungles of Vietnam, Korea and Kuwait, the Holocaust and Hiroshima. There are orphans in Israel still and widows in Palestine and Irish hearts are broken on all sides of its borders. In African tribes, parents watch their children starve. Litanies of sorrow, from the continents and the seas, echoing from pole to pole, resonating around the equator. A planet wrapped in anguish of its own making.

Why don't we get it right? With so much at stake, why have we not done better?

There is no hope for us until our humanity is fully engaged. We ourselves are the image and likeness of God. Not the church. Not religion. Not the State.

We are the sacraments. and we celebrate them by living. The other sacraments are rituals, valuable, irreplaceable, but less than ourselves.

Whenever the Church retreats to the rituals and ignores humanity, it wages war on its own people. The norm for sacramental celebration is not orthodoxy but a life fully lived.

The reign of God is within us. We were told that a long time ago. Ministers of the Church denied this and insisted that the Church was sacred and humanity profane. Ministers of State decreed that people are expendable when policies are urgent, that wars and starving times are in order when the issue is right.

Why is it self indulgent to seek God within, if that is where God chooses to dwell?

Jesus finds God, not in the Temple but in the inner sanctuary of his own being.

Human systems, religious or mundane, are only as valid as the humanity they bear.

The final deception in all systems of salvation is the illusion that we can be healed by something outside us.

In the deepest recesses of the human heart, there is divinity. Not of our own making. The human heart was not made by us. Then, surely God was not. Divinity is always gift, grace, given.

As we hear the voice of God, deep, deep within us, we hear a human voice. It calls us to put aside our swords. For all who take the sword end the lives of others and their own life. In doing so, they silence the voice of God. To live by violence is the death of the heart. When the heart dies, God is absent.

When the sword is not drawn, even against the enemy, even against those who come for us by night as we pray, then there is peace.

Why does it not get better?

Because we try to find our way without ourselves.

The face of God is not strange. It is familiar.

We find God in every human face.

We miss God when we suppose that God could not look so much like us.

WITNESS

It happened on this side of the Jordan, we are told.

It was the last time he bore witness. A good man. One of the best. Fading. Melancholy and miracles.

I am, he says, the bridegroom's friend. The best friend, the best man, perhaps. Watching at the door of the bride's house. Waiting for the bridegroom to arrive here and marry the bride.

I watch. I wait. Not for me. For someone else. I stand. I listen. How I long to hear!

When, at long last, or so it seems, the voice of the bridegroom is heard, the friend is overjoyed.

It is, of course, John, of whom we speak. A baptizer. A clearer of rough roads. A voice raised in the wilderness. A reed not shaken by the wind. A prophet. More than a prophet. A friend of the bridegroom.

You see, John observes, I am the one who hears the voice of the groom and steps aside.

Everything is in that stepping aside. It is done partly in humility but mostly in joy. All that the friend wishes is that the bridegroom be celebrated. Humility is never very good without joy.

"The same joy the friend feels, I feel", John tells us. I was called to wait, to watch, to listen, to rejoice, to step aside. My joy is complete now. Complete. I could not be more happy.

The bridegroom of whom we speak if, of course, the Lamb of God, the Messiah we longed for, the Savior we feared would never come, the only–begotten of the Light. Light from Light.

And, I, I was a witness for the light. Not the light. Just a witness. And that was enough for me. It was, already, more than anyone could want. To have borne witness to the light. To have waited for the light and seen it. Is not this all that life could possibly bring?

Some bear witness to the darkness. Or they suppose they are the light—which is, of course, another form of darkness. The true light shines in the darkness. And the darkness cannot overpower it.

I was not that, John says.

I never thought I was the light. A light no darkness could touch. I was not that.

And, then, John speaks words which sum up a lifetime and echo through the centuries with their grandeur and their challenge.

"He must increase; I must decrease."

Words of love in its purest form.

"He must increase; I must decrease."

Every parent who bears a child in love, every pastor who serves a community with affection, every teacher who nurtures a student in hope–all know that others must grow even if they themselves are less.

In the decrease, in the lessening, there is joy and peace, and humility and magnanimity, and freedom and grace, and light. So much light.

In the crucified darkness of Calvary, the Messiah surrenders to the greatness of God, to the light beyond the darkness. Sometimes the light is impossible to see. And we find our way through the darkness only by faith. God must increase even if I be less. To die for the light. Is that not everything?

The last cry from the cross, in the darkness, is surrender. I trusted you. Into your hands, I give everything. I am nothing now. It is only in the final surrender, when nothing is left to give, that the limitless light dawns.

There is no Easter until God is the only source of light. Easter does us no good until we have learned to step aside. Humility only counts if it is done in joy.

All of this happened on this side of the Jordan, we are told.

The baptisms. The preaching. The voice in the wilderness. The arrival of the bridegroom. Even the sadness. The cross. Melancholy and miracles. But also Easter.

Most of all, the light. The light before whom we are darkness. The light which makes us its own.

Before the light, the darkness willingly relents. In becoming less, the darkness is more.

Baptism and Easter. One now. The friend hears the bridegroom. On this side of the Jordan.

Oh Rabboni! Humility in joy. We were taught by John to listen, to wait, to watch. And now our joy is complete. For we have just found everything.

GETHSEMANE

The death squads came at night, armed, lethal. There was no escape. They sought those who struggled for justice and mourned its loss, who hungered for decency and called for mercy, the children of God, peace–makers in a time of turbulence. The death squads were the angel of death in lands where there was no Passover reprieve, no safety zones from violence.

It was much the same that fateful night when they arrested Jesus for blasphemy and sedition. Blasphemy is a ready word to hurl against those who violate violent systems sanctioned by law. Sedition is a convenient charge to level against those who destabilize oppressive structures entrenched by force.

They came, we are told, with clubs and swords and lanterns. A large crowd, Matthew reports. In their midst was a friend of the accused convinced he was saving the condemned man from his own excesses. Treachery seeks reasons to justify the unjustifiable.

The Nazis, we know, came by night with loud knocks and shrill shouts, with weapons and flashlights, always in a crowd. Then, too, the charges were blasphemy and sedition against the pure blood of Aryan superiority and the millennial promises of the Third Reich.

In Soviet Russia, the KGB sent soldiers by night following the same pattern, issuing the same charges.

Violence is never creative. It repeats the past. It has no hope. It feeds on terror.

Abductors come by night for the accused when the charges have no substance, hiding their identity, sometimes their shame, in the darkness. Judas was known. It was, therefore, only his shame he covered.

Treachery seeks reasons but never finds them.

If the charges are substantial, if the cause is right, all is done in the open.

"I sat daily with you in the Temple, teaching, and you did not lay hands on me." And now, Jesus says, "you have come as against a robber."

Temple police and death squads come by night fortifying corrupt institutions, ecclesiastical or secular, by the slaughter of the innocent.

The Temple police this night arrest a man most people consider the most innocent man who ever lived. Death squads killed children in this hemisphere as a means of intensifying terror; in the camps, children were gassed first. Innocence is inconvenient, threatening, to systems which crush the human spirit.

It is more than ritual we repeat every paschal season. It is history. We remember because the present will not let us forget. The innocent have been put to death in such astonishing numbers, from Gethsemane to Auschwitz, from Bethlehem to Tiannamen

Square, from slavery to segregation, in racist circles and tribal massacres, from Abel to Romero, from Imperial Rome to impoverished El Salvador, at the stake and in the gulags, on crosses from Calvary to the Berlin Wall.

The arrest of Jesus is unforgettable because he teaches Peter during it that his disciples must not draw their swords. In disarming Peter, Jesus disarms every Christian. At least that was the intent.

We would have lived in a vastly different world if Christianity had given itself whole–heartedly to the banishment of all weapons, from the beginning, with no exceptions allowed. If it was not right to use a weapon to save Jesus from a horrible death, how could it be right to employ violence to protect the church? Christianity's most glorious centuries and most impressive saints were non–violent.

Christianity could have made such a difference in teaching the human family non–violence. Because it did not and does not, we weep for the loss of the innocent and the kiss of betrayal.

EMPTY PROMISES

The cross is empty now. May it always be so.

Death is sometimes an act of gratitude, Eucharist in another form. There is no Eucharist without death, no broken bread without a broken heart, no wine of deliverance until the last breath of life is the first gift of the Spirit.

How can such opposites be reconciled? Death is the other side of life and yet its necessary center. Even the God of life is an abstraction until God dies. And, then, God is inescapable, buried in the deepest levels of human history, like seed not yet wheat.

Death makes Advent vigils of our lives, compelling us to await its arrival.

We want so much to keep life as we have known it. We would permit no loved one to go. The agony in such a loss has no name. It can only be felt as it tears up all the securities and leaves us in shreds. We would permit no loved one to go. And we ourselves are not eager to depart. The first savior we seek is the one who can rescue us from the death we cannot abide. We should be grateful our search is in vain. Such a savior would bring safety by confining us to a life of such limitations. All securities eventually imprison us, lock out the future, incarcerate us in the present. Prisoners of despair. Sooner or later total security in the present would unsettle us with fear about a different future and with those who might propose it. Eventually we would be frightened of our own capacity to generate new dreams, fresh visions.

Had we been given the choice, we would have kept Jesus as we once knew him. Death is not a choice but a necessity, like birth. Strange that our lives of choice begin and end with necessities.

The disciples plead with Jesus to stay. He was able, they believed, to do signs and wonders. Why would he not do this?

Is not death somehow a betrayal of friendship, the ultimate act of infidelity in a marriage? Is not the death of a parent the cruelest form of child abuse? Does not death make all love provisional and somehow unbelievable? If you leave me when I need your most, if your leave me when I cannot find my way without you and I can never know where you have gone, how is that love?

Without death, we would not easily believe life had any other possibilities beyond its present form. The ultimate act of faith is to see possibilities in emptiness. Absence makes apostates of us all. At least in the first experience of it. Presence makes us believers, especially when it is in the void that we affirm the presence.

The empty cross is such an ambiguous symbol. We have learned little in this century if we have not understood that ambiguity is the way certitude manifests itself to sensitive and loving people.

The empty cross creates gratitude. We are grateful that the

200

agony and the pain have stopped. We never knew how much torment the human heart could bear before all the life is shaken out
of it. We are grateful that the crucified is, at long last, taken down,
that the hopeless search for comfort on the cross is finished. We
are, nonetheless, grateful with regrets. Death raises questions about
whether it was avoidable.

There is no Eucharist until the cross is empty. The Last Supper
is only a ritual without an empty cross. Life is play acting without
death, a scene that goes on endlessly even when its purpose is no
longer apparent. Love is theater if we are not willing to die for the
other. True love exhausts life and takes all we have, a candle struggling to give light until its substance disappears.

Death is love's first journey into the future. Those who precede
us into death bring us into a new future, first by our grief, then by
our faith, finally in gratitude. The death of someone we love makes
us want to die, too, not in hopelessness but in anticipation of new
possibilities.

The cross is empty now. They tell us the tomb was empty also.
Easter finds possibilities, presence, in emptiness. Easter is a form
emptiness takes when it is time for the present to pass. Until we lose
everything, we cling to the present. We cannot give ourselves fully to
the future while clutching the present. Emptiness, first, then, Easter.

There is no birth without an empty womb. There is no
Eucharist without an empty cross. There is no Easter until our
hearts are so desperately empty that only the Spirit can fill them.

Then, there are Alleluias everywhere, shouts of joy only the
future creates. Christ walks on all the Emmaus roads of our lives
and calls us from the shore of every sea. Easter, then, descends upon
us in the winds and flame of Pentecost and we find communion
with Christ in the endless Eucharist of a life that now has nothing
to fear.

We know we have met the Easter Christ not because we can
touch and hold and cling to what was or is, as in a certitude. We
know the Easter Christ because the fears are gone and the future is

alive with transparency, presence, and life. The present becomes provisional. Easter empties all the tombs, rolls back all impossibilities, eludes the burial cloths of the present and fills the earth with angels of hope.

CROSSES IN THE EARLY DARKNESS

PRIEST, A MOVIE

A Struggle for Faith and Mission

Two of the most troubling questions disturbing Catholicism are issues concerning how we get our sexuality right and where we find the proper balance between authority and license. They are not easy questions to answer. Catholicism today does not do a good job addressing these problems nor, we might add, does the world at large. *PRIEST* raises both questions in a film whose power and pain make it a modern Passion Play.

The film was originally scheduled for release on Good Friday. Whatever the motive, there is a haunting aptness about that initial decision. This is a film about a rush to judgment and a crucifixion. It is about a crowd jeering as a man's life is being taken from him and about a woman who, Pieta fashion, holds him in her arms when no one else will claim him. It is a Good Friday story challenging us to define what we believe the ultimate obscenities in life are, confronting us with questions of what is left when all the initial dreams and ideals are lost, forcing us to state whether or not we can hope for pity and redemption in those moments when we feel most unworthy of them.

This is not an easy film. It is a Passion story, stark and naked, assaulting our categories of all that is sacred and legitimate in an effort to encounter what is finally worthwhile in the priesthood, the

205

church and life itself. It is no wonder that the film is controversial. It pits two churches, two spiritualities, two definitions of priesthood against each other.

There is much here to explain.

We said, in the beginning that we need to get our sexuality right. If we do not, something about our authenticity and integrity, about holiness and wholeness is lost.

PRIEST gives us the story of four priests who settle the question of sexuality in four different ways. We need to choose which of these we believe is true and in accord with the gospel. It will not be obvious. The film makes the issues raw and it sometimes lapses into caricature as it presents them but it keeps the issues before us, challenging, almost taunting, but always probing.

Matthew, the pastor of an inner city parish, has been called to priesthood, that is clear, but not to celibacy. We might argue about whether he should have known that before he became a priest and we might question whether the arrangement that he and Maria, his housekeeper, makes is proper. These questions are incidental to the central issue of whether or not he has been called to be a priest and whether or not he brings Christ to his people in a compelling manner. Maria tells the conservative young priest who comes to assist Matthew and who is offended by the sexual relationship, that Matthew wishes to marry her but that she will not allow him to leave the ministry because it will break his heart and wither his spirit. Does one surrender a priesthood which is God–given and healing to people for a law which came late in church history and which is man–made, in all senses of that word? Does the church lose when people like Matthew resign? Does God, so to speak, lose when commitments, to Maria or to priesthood, are broken by those who abandon the women they love or resign the ministry to which they have been called? Where are the deeper fidelities here? What is the compassionate, human thing to do? Have we divorced the gospel so much from humanity that questions about human decency seem to dilute the gospel?

The unnamed pastor of a rural parish is chosen to rehabilitate Greg, the young homosexual priest, after his life and reputation unravel. This pastor has kept the law and made his decision for celibacy at all costs. He is celibate but there is no priesthood left in him. He is a type we all have known. In presenting him, the film lapses into caricature. The pastor is sadistic, sexually repressed, mechanical. He speaks Latin better than English communicating in a language no living people use. To present such a priest is not to say that all priests who are celibate lose their humanity. Nor is it to declare that celibacy cannot enrich priesthood. It clearly does and has. But for many priests this does not happen. If it did, why would tens of thousands resign? The pastor is dead and yet he is legal; he has no heart and yet he is supported by the institutional church in every way. He has settled his sexuality by destroying his life and by assaulting the vulnerable, especially the sexually vulnerable, whom he envies and tortures.

The bishop represents a third way of seeking to get sexuality right. He too is not well drawn. He is a stereotype and there is no ambiguity, no saving graces in his personality. There are bishops who are different, men who suffer with people and, shepherd like, seek them out when they are lost. The film did not present such a bishop, not because it says they do not exist but because there are fewer of them than the church needs. The bishop in this film knows the beauracratic requirements of the institution. He sacrifices his sexuality on the altar of career and promotion. One gets it perfectly when he comes to visit Greg who has attempted suicide after his conviction for what the law calls, ungraciously, lewd, public behavior. The bishop enters the hospital, pursued by reporters, telling them that we, he, all of us, must be compassionate. He says the right things, even brings flowers. Alone with the priest, he rejects him savagely. He is disappointed Greg survived the suicide attempt, demanding now that he get out of his diocese. This is not a father holding a sobbing prodigal son in his arms but a tormentor who will execute people if need be to preserve his power. Jesus once declared that those who kill the body are less pernicious than those who kill the spirit. The bishop is a soul-slayer, a life taker, a judge who, as Nazi judges once did, will render any verdict his superiors require.

It is in Greg that the issue of sexuality is most controversial. He has to be a homosexual for the film to work; the main protagonist must take sexuality into deeply disturbing and censured areas for its message to be clear. In the beginning of the film, Greg is cold, judgmental, rigidly orthodox. He dislikes Maria, patronizes Matthew, preaches to people a message they neither need nor understand. At this point, he is blessed by the institution, even possibly on a fast career track.

Maria changes him when she tells him that she loves Matthew's priesthood more than her happiness, that she loves Matthew more than herself, and, therefore, will not allow Matthew to do what he passionately wants more than anything else, namely, marry her. She tells Greg that while he despises her she is cleaning his laundry, washing dishes and preparing meals.

Greg might have remained celibate, his homosexuality in check so to speak, had the loneliness of the priesthood not become more than he could bear. The loneliness of priesthood is not the loneliness all of us must live through if we are to be mature or authentic. It is the loneliness of those who sense that they can never have a life of their own and that their deepest needs as human beings must be denied if they are to function in the system. This loneliness is not the burden all priests bear but it is the burden many of them do. If they did not, the Catholic priesthood would be in a healthy state. Does anyone really believe it is anymore?

To say this is not to deny that there are many good and happy priests.

Greg watches Matthew and Maria share a common life together. He longs for the companionship he is denied. One night he overhears their conversation and their laughter and he is as bereft as he has ever been. He goes to a gay bar and engages in what he intends to be a one–night stand. The eroticism, however, touches his soul and demands commitment from him. To say that this happens to Greg is not to say that it happens to all priests. Not all priests are homosexual, most are not. Not all priests find commitment through eroticism but many people do. Should the film maker be forbidden to show that this clearly happens to people, many people, because there are critics who are offended by the reality before them?

The homosexual scenes are graphic and it is here that the film will disturb most people. I believe the explicitness is necessary to show the physical, sexual experience which brings Greg to a deeper sense of priesthood. Those who are troubled by homosexual or explicit sex might ask themselves whether these are the ultimate obscenities in the film, in life, in the church.

I find PRIEST most compellingly Catholic in its effort to situate the priesthood in sacrament rather than law. Catholics have always had a deep sacramental consciousness. The drama of this film centers around how one evaluates the sacraments of priesthood, Reconciliation and Eucharist.

It is clear that the film makes no sense unless one believes ordination is sacred. The title of the film makes it unmistakable that the film has no meaning if priesthood does not. The message on priesthood is hopeful for those who have eyes to see and ears to hear. The message is simply this, the priesthood holds and people choose it, indeed are willing to give their lives to it and for it, even though it may crucify and break them. As Matthew and Greg become more human, they opt for priesthood even more strongly. One of the saddest men in the film is a priest we have not discussed. He is an older, alcoholic associate priest whom Greg replaced on his first assignment. This priest lost his commitment to priesthood and is unable to recover, both because his priesthood is gone and because the celibacy he has lived has made him realize that the church stole his life from him when it had no right to and when there was no need. For sacrifice and the cross to matter, there must be no other options. In his case, in the case of many priests, there are. The film begins with this priest carrying a huge crucifix to the bishop's mansion and running it through the window. It is an apt portrayal of a crucifixion demanded when it was not required. The shattered glass is a symbol of the shattered lives the institution sometimes leaves in its wake.

The sacrament of Reconciliation roots this story in perhaps its most dramatic episode. A young girl confesses to Greg that she is being sexually abused by her father. She is a sullen, wounded angel whose sexual experience is dictated by her father much as the sexual definitions of priests in this film are settled not by themselves but by a patriarchal institution. It is she who, in the end, embraces the broken priest and rescues him. This episode is presented with all the force of Dante's *Inferno*. Her father is a man whose evil is so palpable that it terrifies. His face, distorted by the confessional grille, is as distorted as his sexuality. His face is the face of evil itself.

Greg cannot find a way to rescue the young girl without breaking the confessional seal. He prays in his room for guidance as he has never prayed before. In this Gethsemane scene he weeps and cries out in terror, blasphemy, and anger. The explicitness of this denunciation of God by a priest is as necessary as the earlier sexual scenes. One cannot understand the goodness and anguish of Greg's heart, the passion and depth of his priesthood, the power and need of his love for people unless this scene is as harsh as it is. Losing control for the sake of love is what makes Greg a priest in the fullest sense of the word.

In affirming these qualities in the film, we are not condoning the sometimes aberrant behavior of these priests or other priests. We merely note that many people come to God by walking crooked lines. Why is it we are troubled more by sexual behavior against the rules than by heartless celibacy? Are not both problems? Greg feels remorse; the cadaverous pastor of a rural parish never does.

Sooner or later, all Catholic theology and life, indeed all definitions of priesthood, return to Eucharist. This film contains, perhaps, the most powerful Communion scene I have ever experienced. Matthew invites Greg to concelebrate Eucharist with him after Greg has been dismissed by his bishop, denounced in the press, denied by his parishioners, detained by the police, deserted by the church. The Eucharist is Matthew's effort at reconciliation between this bereft priest and the institution that needs to love him. It also becomes an affirmation of the priesthood before the doubting and divided congregation. In Eucharist all the sacraments are brought to fulfillment. As the body of Christ is consecrated in faith and broken, Greg begins to weep, for the consecration he fears he has lost, for the fragments of a life he cannot put together. He, like Christ on the cross, bleeds from every wound and hears only hate from people whom he needs. He looks for someone, anyone, to convince him before he dies that he has not lived in vain. Matthew asks his congregation to make sense of the crucifixion of their brother, to speak a word of love, to rescue him with new life and Easter hope. Many walk away. During communion, no one will receive Christ from Greg. He stands alone with the consecrated body of Christ in his hands. He cannot be a priest unless someone takes Christ from his hands, from his priesthood.

All the parishioners stand in line to receive Communion from Matthew only, a priest who is also broken but who has not been legally rejected by the institution. At long last, the young girl whose father abused her comes foreword. It was for her that a miracle had been accomplished when Greg lost his faith and found God in the Gethsemane scene where he prayed from the very bones and blood of his life. The film ends as these two utterly lost souls whom many would condemn to the *Inferno* sob, giving communion to each other from all the wounds of their lives. This reverse Pieta has the woman redeem the priest and preserve him from death by her act of compassion and courage.

A half century ago, Graham Greene wrote a powerful novel, **The Power and the Glory,** about a priest who lost his way. It was a story for a different church, a church before Vatican II. In it, the priest is guilt–ridden because he cannot measure up to the ideals of the priesthood and the church. Sex and alcohol rob him of his priesthood, his sense of consecration and innocence, his ability to see himself as authentic. At the end, his belief in sacraments and his courage lead him to give his life for another. *The Power and the Glory* is a story about the power of the sacraments and the glory of the church. Sacraments have the power to function so effectively that God seems almost confined to them. Indeed, priesthood is defined so much in terms of ordination that all else is secondary to it. Analogously, it would be like making far more of the wedding than the marriage.

PRIEST is a post–Vatican II *Power and the Glory.* Here it is not only the priest who is broken but the church as well. The power and the glory belong to God. Both the priest and the church are rescued by God alone.

The continuity in faith between the church of *Power and the Glory* and the church of *PRIEST* is our faith in sacraments, priesthood and, ultimately in God and in Christ. An alcoholic priest in Greene's novel disturbed people as now a homosexual priest does. The ultimate scandal, however, is to believe that God is less than our problems and somehow dependent on our sacraments, rules and even good behavior.

The fugitive priest in *The Power and the Glory* and the priests in *PRIEST*, we should know, are good priests if they love and give their lives to people. All else is incidental and faithless. In both stories, the central priest character knows he is not morally fit to celebrate the Eucharist and yet both are compellingly called by Christ to be at the table. They come to learn that Communion is very important but that compassion is much more. And so there are continuities between the two churches.

It is the sacrament of humanity and the people who bring us grace which define the difference between life and death. The fugitive priest in Greene's novel knows this but he still supposes that humanity is not much good without sacraments and priesthood. Mexico, in Greene's story, as it excludes the priesthood, becomes corrupt and repulsive. The world is very little without the church. In *PRIEST*, however, sacraments take on meaning from the people who receive them. The church is not much good without humanity. Grace abides in people who find their way to God even if priests are not there to guide them. And yet priests matter.

In the final scene of *PRIEST*, it is not a priest, as in **The Power and the Glory**, who rescues a dying lay person but a lay person, a woman, no longer a virgin, who rescues a priest. In this, one sees all the difference between the church of another age and the church of our age. In the priesthood of all believers, anyone, everyone, may be priest when the institution will not ordain or support those who are. This could never have happened in Greene's church.

The sense of duty and responsibility for the salvation of the world is given to priests in Greene's novel. It is the church's business. In *PRIEST*, the housekeeper rescues the young priest (unthinkable in pre–Vatican II Catholicism, especially a housekeeper who sleeps with the pastor); a homosexual lover demands commitment from a priest whose first instinct is to treat him as a casual experience.

The most powerful scene of all occurs in the final moments, as we have said. A young women, betrayed by her father and crucified on his bed of lust, walks down the aisle to take Christ from the hands of a priest only Christ and hardly anyone else seems to accept. She becomes in that instant a redeemer rather than a victim. It is she who bears the power and the glory. Better, it is the two of them who make up the church, no one less essential than the other. She is the new church, the new People of God, if you will, still searching for priesthood and church and willing to accept them wherever humanity is not denied, compassion betrayed and Christ marginalized. She could not be fully healed without this priest's literally miraculous love for her; he might attempt suicide again except for the love of people like her who will not let him or his priesthood be destroyed. The priesthood is not only God's work but the work of God's People.

If this is the new church, it is not always a church of power and glory. It is as messy at times as Peter's betrayal and apostolic doubt and the early church's confusion. It is as far removed from glory as a prodigal son and a woman caught in adultery. The young woman, only fourteen, in the final scene of *PRIEST* holds the sobbing priest in her arms after he has given her the Eucharist. Both know how shameful their lives have been. Both know how much they want and need Christ. The young woman, we have said, becomes a redeemer rather than a victim. There is more. She becomes a redeemer because she is a victim. It is the essential story of the cross and of Good Friday. It is a task we have all been given. Is it not?

PRIEST, A MOVIE

A HOMILY:
FOR MY MOTHER
On the Occasion of the Funeral

There is something eternal about a mother.

I remember the beginning of all the major events of my life: school, graduation. friendship. ordination, marriage. children, career. I don't remember the beginnings of my relationship with my mother. She always was, it seems. For me, Mary my mother, was eternal. She was always there.

If our relationships with our mothers are good, then this becomes our first experience of eternal love.

The death of a mother is like being told eternity does not last or that eternal love has limits. None of this is logical but all of it is experiential.

The church to which we belong calls itself Mother church. The awareness we have of our mothers helps us define what that means and what the church is. We who labor for a renewed church do so because we want the church to be worthy of being called our Mother.

There is more than this.

It is in our mother's arms that we first see the face of God.

The death of a mother, and of such a mother, brings everything

217

in our lives to crisis.

We learn so many lessons, so many life parables, from our mothers. I learned from Mary how to forgive and how to love. All those who followed her taught me lessons of less significance and of less importance.

In our mother's wombs and from their breasts. we take communion for the first time. Every priest who repeats the immortal words: "This is my Body; This is my Blood" evokes not only the memory of Jesus but the mystery of motherhood itself. The first one to give us her body and blood is our mother.

And, so, a mother is a sacramental experience.

All of this seems to be ending now. The death of our mother is also a death of me and my sister. Nothing will ever be the same again after this.

Tonight is not a season of wholeness but a time to gather the fragments of our lives. Death splinters and shatters our lives and leads us to suppose that healing and wholeness are no longer possible. We gather what is left in the hope that the pieces might come together in a new pattern and help us to make sense of life once more. Tonight that does not seem possible. But tonight is only tonight.

The passing of a mother makes everything conditional, puts everything in one's life on hold. and creates a fear that everything is provisional and even valueless. It had to have been that way at the cross for both the mother and the son.

Mothers are the angels of compassion God sends us when we doubt the meaning of ourselves and of our lives. It is not easy for us when the angel is gone. But angels are not made for this world alone.

After a death, and such a death, we gather the fragments of our lives together and try to find a use for them. As children we brought our mothers the shards and shells, the flowers and stones we found in our small world. We all did that, as an act of tribute and a gesture of gratitude. Our mothers always made sense of them and fashioned a meaning from these worthless treasures, making them priceless in their acceptance of them and in the joy it gave them.

Who now will make the poor treasures of our lives rich with meaning?

Hope is no easy word at a time like this.

Mary, my mother. was a woman of such extraordinary gifts that I came to believe she was everlasting. I could imagine my own death more easily than hers. Of course, I knew with my mind there was a time limit to her life but I denied it in my heart and soul.

How could such a woman pass away? Where would all that love and all that grace and all that gentleness and all that life go?

Today she is gone and a great deal of who I am is with her. Her life ended gently as she grew weaker going out like a candle after all the substance of her life was spent.

Of all the stirring memories of her I have, the one that has recurred most often in these weeks is the memory of her standing with the other mothers outside Holy Cross School in Harrison at the end of our school day ready to walk me and my sister home. Her face and her arms brought us home before we ever reached our house.

We have come together tonight to pay tribute and to give honor. I thank God for the first woman I ever loved, the woman who made all other loves possible. I cannot think of what to add to that.

She told me, in the final weeks, she would never leave those she loved. Jesus once said the same to his friends. And Christ is still with us. And so I trust with all my heart that my mother's words will prove equally valid. Otherwise the remainder of the journey will be less bearable.

Jesus left us to become the Christ not only for a few but for all.

Perhaps my mother can now be a mother for more than my sister and me. I would wish such a mother for every child in this world. For then all the children of the world would be safe and blessed.

Today we sing a song to Mary Padovano, not a sad song although we are broken by grief. No, we sing a Magnificat. Mary of Nazareth's hymn was filled with joy and expansiveness. So was my mother's life. And so tears do not become her. I do not remember her as weeping but as exuberant and vibrant.

In the gospel reading, we heard Jesus call another Mary in the garden on Easter morning. Her response was also filled with joy and expansiveness.

And so I struggle tonight to find joy in the broken pieces of my life. If I do not I will miss my mother and her spirit.

I know my mother wants my sister and me to find an expansive spirit in this sorrow, to sing a Magnificat and to believe in the Easter mystery of life invincible. This is what my faith and my mother taught me.

Tonight I ask God to gather the broken pieces of my mother's life, the fragments of her body, and to make them whole again. My hand is too small for such a gathering.

But if God does this, if I believe God does this, I shall have hope. And one day I shall see the face of God again in my mother's arms.

A HOMILY, MARY ROSE CIERZO PADOVANO

MARRIED PRIESTS:

ISSUES AND ANSWERS

Top Ten criticisms!

Many *CORPUS* members are in dialogue with their bishops and church leaders; they are often interviewed by the press, radio and television. The following ten criticisms have surfaced with some regularity.

1. *Married priests are men of broken commitments and sources of scandal.*

It is a tradition in our church to affirm that sacraments are for people (sacramenta propter homines); we believe this is also true for vows and promises. We do not mean by this that vows and promises are to be taken lightly anymore than we would take sacraments lightly. A vow, however, always needs to be seen in a life context. Our church recognizes this by allowing annulments and separations in marriages and by releasing people form commitments to celibacy and religious life.

We believe that a promise no longer kept should be subject to consequences and that the official church should not dispense too readily from serious commitments. But we also maintain that endlessly to punish or penalize someone who did not continue on a path once chosen is not in accord with the gospel. At some point, we are all obliged to relent and to reconcile, especially with a person who is faithful in other areas of life and remains committed to priesthood and church.

Is it naïve to ask what Jesus would have done with married priests? Would he see marriage as an impediment in his service? The impediment is the marriage for many and not the broken promise since priests whose wives have died are received back readily even though the promise is just as broken. When the New Testament has Jesus ask disciples to give up families and children, he surely did not mean that all disciples must be celibate, or that all the better disciples must be. Had this been true, our church would never have developed its beautiful theology of marriage or declared it a sacrament. It is devotion and forgiveness and love which mark us out as disciples of Jesus and not a particular state of life. In any case, we ask whether the church might not annul the promise of celibacy for the sake of preserving a priest's ministry, just as it annuls marriages. The church annuls marriage even though the end of a "marriage" is a very different and a far more demanding change than the annulment of a law of celibacy the church created on its own initiative. Divorce, annulment and dispensation from celibacy have almost nothing in common and should not be simply equated.

Nevertheless, an "annulment" of the promise of celibacy represents an easier change than annulment of marriage and is all the more fitting when the church does this for the sake of its own people who are served by too few pastors. In this instance, the church would invite the candidate to start anew and would monitor the priest's ministry to see if people and bishops find it acceptable.

It is important, of course, not to scandalize people, but we all know that some people are scandalized whenever compassion or forgiveness occurs. The elder son in the parable of the lost or prodigal son would have been more comfortable with punishment or vindictiveness or so the darker side of his nature supposed.

Do we bring the best out of people when we encourage them to think harshly of their former pastoral leaders? If some people turn from the church or from Christ because married priests are readmitted, if they are less faithful to their marriages because of this reinstatement, one wonders where their priorities are and whether such attitudes should be corrected.

Is it possible that the greater scandal is the dismissal of 100,000 priests from their ministries in a twenty–year period? Is it not a scandal for the laity to see the church as unforgiving and willing to punish a priest until his death supposing thereby that we honor God and save people the bad witness of reconciliation with those we deem unworthy?

2. There is no tradition of marriage after ordination; we now ordain married men who are converts or in celibate marriages in the Latin Rite; one day we might expand this pastoral provision, but both traditional and ecumenical sensitivity to the Eastern Orthodox churches would lead us to exclude priests who marry on their own initiative.

Most bishops reject the ordination of married men even though we have a long tradition in this regard, one with explicit New Testament support (letters to Timothy and Titus; Peter's marriage; Paul's acceptance of married apostles and ministers). And, so, the issue may not be tradition.

All would agree that this tradition of no marriage after ordination does not derive from Christ or the Apostles. Priests did continue to minister as priests even after they married in former centuries.

In any case, the records from the Fathers of the church and from the Councils and Synods of the first millennium show that marriage and women and sexual expression even for the sake of children, were judged almost always sinful. Since the celibate priesthood was supposed to be a higher form of Christian life, one was reluctantly allowed to go from marriage (an inferior state) to priesthood (a superior state) but not from priesthood (a superior state) to marriage (an inferior state). This reasoning is no longer acceptable in the church; it would be rejected in our preaching and pastoral practice; and it has no endorsement from the Second Vatican Council.

There is no New Testament support for allowing us to regard marriage as praiseworthy before ministry and blameworthy after it has begun. How could we ever present or defend such a contrived chronological sequence without feeling embarrassed by the reasoning which supports it?

We respect the decision of the Bishop of Rome and his brother bishops to conclude that it is pastorally better to have an exclusively celibate priesthood in the Latin Rite when conversion and celibate marriage are not valid exceptions. We believe, however, that this policy causes enormous damage to Christian communities by making less available to them pastoral care, Eucharistic and sacramental life, and the witness of marriage which a married priest gives in a special way.

Even if one might argue that married priests in the Eastern Rite and in the other Christian churches are not better than celibate priests, one would not conclude that they are worse and that marriage has made them worse. Who would say such a thing? If those marred priests, who have an option to marry or not, are not worse but just as good, then what does mandatory celibacy accomplish in terms of ministry? Was the celibate Paul a better apostle than the married Peter? Did not the Christian community love both and learn from both? Is it not their devotion to Christ which moves us in these apostles rather than their marital status?

We need to do what we believe proper in our tradition even if the Orthodox churches do not fully endorse this. Their tradition of no marriage after ordination is built on a model of optional celibacy which gives candidates a choice before ordination. A reunited Christian church would have room for different Rites as is now the case with respect to marriage and priesthood in the Eastern Rite and the Latin Rite Catholic communities.

Married priests are asking for nothing more than the privilege of serving the church and God's People. The agenda and intent are as simple as that.

3. *CORPUS is opposed to celibacy and not unwilling to comment on problems which some canonical celibate priests encounter.*

CORPUS has never denigrated celibacy when it is clearly the choice and option of the minister. Celibacy was also a choice married priests once made, a choice many of us may have chosen even if an option had been available. It is a choice, furthermore, made by many of our brothers and friends, a choice our sisters and family members make in their religious communities. To demean celibacy would be to distance ourselves from people we treasure and to favor mandatory marriage.

We know that celibacy works for many priests and that they chose it for the best of reasons. We have neither the right not the inclination to diminish the luster of their lives and the witness of their work.

If *CORPUS* comments on the scandals which some priests encounter, it is only when we are asked if there is a connection between the way this behavior emerges in the church and mandatory celibacy. The case for a married priesthood does not need failures in the celibate priesthood to be persuasive. We are not naïve enough to presume that a married priesthood will eliminate immoral behavior and we know that a married priesthood will bring new problems with it such as divorce and loveless marriages. Nevertheless, studies by Dean Hoge of the Catholic University of America, show that the sexual problems of married clergy in other churches are less severe than the current status of sexual problems of celibate clergy in the Catholic church.

We believe that mandatory celibacy harms the church more than it serves it. Archbishop Weakland of Milwaukee comments in the July 22, 1991 *New York* that "across the board, celibacy works to our detriment as a church." We seek a change in the law not because this will remove all problems, but because we think that such a change will serve the People of God better and will burden the priesthood less. A married priesthood makes it likely that we can have parishes of more manageable size. We know from our experience that priests do not work harder in pastoral ministry because they are unmarried; devotion to people is not a consequence of one's marital choices but of the condition of one's heart and of the freedom one has to pursue the life choices consonant with one's calling.

We wish also to affirm, we who have been both celibate and married, that marriage is an inexhaustible spiritual resource and that family life is a graced event of impressive magnitude. We can say this after years of marriage with all its concrete problems as well as happiness. To eliminate this value form the priesthood is unnecessary and unwise.

4. *CORPUS is less interested in others and in the church than it is in its agenda; it wants priesthood on its terms and seeks to regain the status priesthood confers.*

It would be foolish to pretend we are immune to selfishness and mixed motives, to narrow vision and sometimes self–interest. There is hardly a canonical priest who does not suffer at times from the same liabilities. We need redemption and forgiveness and, indeed, acceptance and affirmation.

If self–indulgence were our only motive, we would not have married and raised families. Nor would we continue to offer our service to the church. Nor would we have remained Catholic. We truly believe we were called by God to be priests and we know there are needs in the church we might serve and that these needs will go unmet if priesthood continues to be limited to celibate men.

The *CORPUS* mission pledges us to dialogue about our reinstatement but also to work energetically for a reformed priesthood which would open possibilities for women and for a renewed church with expanded opportunities for collegiality, accountability and spiritual development. Some have criticized us for being politically naïve in asking for more than our reinstatement; and yet to work only for ourselves seems to be self–indulgent and somehow a betrayal of those women, sometimes including our wives and daughters, who desire priesthood as much as we do and who are at least as competent.

We affirm the papal and episcopal structure of the church but also its rich tradition of Eucharist and humanism, of community life and conciliar debate, of diversity of charisms and Catholic inclusiveness.

5. Reinstatement should require exhaustive discernment since some CORPUS members are psychologically wounded, resentful, unreliable, self–seeking and theologically ill–informed.

Some of us are. Some canonical priests and laity, even some bishops and, history tells us, an occasional pope suffered from the same problems. We agree it would be unwise to reinstate dispensed or married priest without careful scrutiny. Ministry remains a privilege rather than a right. A collegial church requires the participation of bishops, the presbyterium and the laity in reinstatement to pastoral appointments.

We believe that most married priests are as healthy psychologically and spiritually as their celibate brothers. Bishops may often see married priest in a less favorable light because we have become accustomed to expect our relationship to be adversarial and uncertain.

There should be a discernment process on a case–by–case basis before readmission. This process would ascertain reliability and theological and pastoral competence. But it may also allow married priests to witness to how the grace of God and the love of their families sustained them, especially in those dark moments when the institutional church denied them and the church they loved tried to recognize them no more. This suffering must not become, however, an excuse for self–pity.

6. *A married priesthood will bring with it divorce, loveless marriage, family and financial pressures, sexual misconduct.*

Indeed, all this will happen since the human condition is fragile and fallible. A church as competent and graced as ours can surely contain the pastoral damage of these losses and prevail in the face of these problems. Celibacy does not bring with it difficulties of lesser magnitude.

The New Testament church did not deny its pastoral leaders marriage although it too experienced these tensions. Neither mandatory celibacy nor sacramental marriage can redeem priests from the faults and flaws of the human condition.

The married priesthood will bring more than burdens with it. It will bring relief from the energy we expend in maintaining mandatory celibacy against the overwhelming clerical and lay support for an option. It will enable us to develop a creative spirituality from the concrete texture of married priesthood. It will give the Catholic community the witness of pastoral leaders who face the same problems they do and create a priestly ministry from them.

A married priesthood may show clearly that service rather than sacrifice or abstinence is the proper model for priesthood. The priest is not as much a sacrificial person as a relational person. The value of sacrifice is not in what one gives up but in whether this makes a difference to others and whether the sacrifice generates greater service.

A substantial change in ministry is frightening for some and we know how much courage it will take to endorse this change. Without this change, however, the priesthood, as we know it, will be diminished.

7. *The reinstatement of married priests will lead to resentment from celibate priests and will create division in the fraternity of the priesthood.*

There will be some resentment. The question is whether the cost of preserving us from this resentment is excessive. To keep 100,000 priests out of priestly ministry, to leave our seminaries empty, to deny our parishes pastors, to refuse God's People a married priesthood, to make the Eucharist unavailable, is a steep price to pay.

There is already resentment among celibate priest because of our departure and that resentment derives not only from our leaving but also from our having been forced to leave. In any case, we may be exaggerating this concern. Married deacons, married convert priests and Eastern Rite married priests have not caused any considerable resentment.

In a real sense, we married priests can appreciate the pain of celibate priests as we walked away from them and the pain of the laity who wanted us to stay and serve them as married priests. Most married priests did not choose to leave their celibate brothers; they were dismissed even though they asked to remain and to serve.

The divisions already exist. The resentment is there whether we are reinstated or not. Perhaps optional celibacy can help us heal the anger as each one makes the choice freely and lives out the blessings and burdens which come from one's own choosing.

8. *We cannot afford a married priesthood financially.*

If all other Christian churches can do this, so can we. Dean Hoge's study on the future of Catholic leadership shows us that the real cost of maintaining a celibate priesthood is fairly close to the average salary paid to clergy in other Christian churches. In our culture, it is probable that the spouse of the married priest would provide a second income for the family.

One of the hidden costs of mandatory celibacy is the large number of priests who resign, the reluctance of canonical priests to recruit, the malaise of those who do not wish to be celibate, the disinterest of young people in celibate priesthood, the disappointment and anger of laity at the deterioration of parish life, the burdens placed on bishops as they face expanding needs and diminished personnel.

An abundance of priests means small parish communities. Sociological studies show that people feel more accepted and volunteer to help in larger numbers when they are part of reasonably sized communities and when they are known well by the pastor and needed for the parish to function.

Some of the most vulnerable people in our church are abandoned because of the priest shortage, those in hospitals, nursing homes, prisons, inner cities and poor rural communities.

Money is important, but it is not so important that it should lead us to deny pastoral leadership and sacraments to our people because of it.

9. *CORPUS is a lobby group and is excessively media—oriented.*

CORPUS is fundamentally an association working for solidarity and healing among married priests. It is also an association hoping for a reformed priesthood and a renewed church. We are a federation of Catholic families, grateful for priesthood and marriage, still defined by our love for the church and by the grace alive in its people.

We do little in terms of being a lobby since we have no access to those structures which directly affect change in the church. We are interested in education and spirituality, in theology and liturgy, in social justice and ministry.

We have made an effort to be responsible and to use accurate data and careful historical research in our media appearances. We have tried to be balanced and hope we have succeeded.

There is no way we can function as the association we are and not attract some media attention. This issue of reforming the church is one of great interest to people. To exclude the media from our public meetings would be a sign that we have something to hide or that we are embarrassed. Neither is true. The reluctance of the American Catholic Bishops and of the Vatican to dialogue with us has made our voice more prophetic and attracted media attention to an issue the Catholic Community wishes to consider. We are grateful for the significant number of cardinals and bishops, presidents of episcopal conferences, who have met with us throughout Asia and Europe.

10. *The call for a married priesthood and for the reinstatement of married priests would be more persuasive if it came from an organization other than CORPUS.*

We agree. If the laity or the bishops asked for a married priesthood, the issue would be resolved quickly. Laity support a reformed ministry and optional celibacy by large majorities; most canonical priests favor the change; many bishops do. No one of these groups has organized nationally around this issue. By default, CORPUS became a voice for an immense voiceless constituency. We do what we prefer not to do until someone else does this for us, themselves and the church at large.

It is not a married or a celibate priesthood which is the ultimate issue but the Christian community.

A CALLING FOR ALL GOD'S PEOPLE
Ten Years of *CORPUS*

As I complete a ten-year tenure as president of *CORPUS*, I would like to review the ten most important changes during that period. I would like to do this in two areas: the structure of *CORPUS* and the spirit of *CORPUS*.

THE STRUCTURE OF *CORPUS*

I list these changes in alphabetical order and leave it to others to assign the priority they would give to selected items.

▷ *The Archives*

The University of Notre Dame invited *CORPUS* in 1993 to preserve its papers in its archives. It did this because of the influence *CORPUS* has had on the history and life of the Unites States Catholic Church.

The Archives have made possible the official history of *CORPUS* now being written by Ralph Bastian and due for publication in 1999.

▷ *The Board*

The Board has been a guiding star for CORPUS. Ten years ago it was selected; it is now an elected Board reflecting the philosophies, constituencies, and regions the membership chooses. Over the last decade, some 26 members have served (currently we have thirteen on the Board). The Board has made CORPUS collegial, gender inclusive and representative. No one person or ideology prevails. One of its more impressive decisions was to include women and laity as members of the Association, Board delegates, and officers. The experience of working with people of such extraordinary dedication and wisdom has brought enlightenment and balance to my life and to the married priest movement.

▷ *Canon Law and Non-Clerical Priesthood*

This 1989 document became a charter empowering married priests to serve God's People with sacramental and pastoral ministry. It helped launch CITI (Celibacy Is The Issue) and has given spiritual comfort to enormous numbers of people.

▷ *Conferences*

There have been eleven national conferences over ten years. From 1988-1998, we met in Washington, D.C., Columbus, San Jose, New York City, Chicago, San Antonio, Washington, D.C. (twentieth anniversary), Kent State, San Diego (jointly with F.C.M., Federation of Christian Ministries), Boston, and Seattle (twenty-fifth anniversary).

Speakers included leaders of the Catholic church and ecumenism in this country: Bernard Cooke, Harvey Cox, Michael Crosby, Thomas Fox, Edwina Gately, Joe Girzone, Richard McBrien, Rosemary Ruether, Tim Unsworth.

Members describe these conferences as pentecostal and re-birth experiences. It is difficult to exaggerate the magnitude and sweep of these annual events.

▷ *Constitution*

The Constitution, approved by national referendum, gave COR-PUS a collegial structure, an elected Board, term limits, an impressive staff system, and full acountability and disclosure.

▷ *Dialogue*

Institutionally, we have dialogued with constituencies in the nation who were in pastoral need and who asked us to stand with them. In addition, we met at a public prayer service and in formal dialogue with the NCCB in 1990 in Santa Clara, California and are currently in dialogue with the U.S.A. bishops at their headquarters in Washington, D.C. We have met formally and publicly with cardinals, presidents and vice presidents of episcopal conferences in Austria, England, Italy and the Philippines. We have met, on a number of occasions, with canonical and celibate priests through the National Federation of Priests Councils and in regional, deanery, and diocesan-wide meetings.

Nationally, CORPUS has been an integral part of COR (Catholic Organizations for Renewal, the national consortium of 30 U.S.A. reform organizations). We have been actively involved since its inception in 1992 and have been present at all its meetings. We supported the massive Gallup Survey on Catholic opinion on reform issues, the national "We Are Church" referendum right through its presentation in Rome, and have participated in two White House meetings.

Internationally, CORPUS was critically active in the foundation of the International Federation of Married Catholic Priests (1986) and has been present at all its executive committee sessions (2 or 3 times a year) and all international meetings of married priests since 1985 (Rome, Netherlands, Spain, Brazil). The CORPUS Ambassador has been vice-president of the Federation since its inception. In 1999, CORPUS will host the first International Congress in the U.S.A., in Atlanta.

CORPUS was also active in the foundation of the newly established "International Movement: We Are Church" and in its recent dialogue with Konrad Raiser, General Secretary of the World Council of Churches.

▷ *Media*

CORPUS has been a fully open association. We have appeared in the media in an overwhelming number of major U.S.A. and international newspapers, magazines, radio interviews and television programs.

We launched *CORPUS* Video, a media resource company, and have supported its innovative programming.

▷ *Publications*

CORPUS REPORTS, produced six times a year, is the flagship of the Association. It brings to the nation and the world groundbreaking theological and pastoral papers and news of married priests and church reform.

We have also published a small library of resources of great merit and worth: wedding services, wake services, legal studies, theological essays and a directory of members.Books are published through *CORPUS COMMUNICATIONS*.

▷ *Regions and Contact*

The regional system has been an object of more analysis and discussion than any other structural issue. We are concerned that contact with members be kept on as personal a basis as the size of our Association allows. Regional coordinators have taken on one of the most demanding ministries in *CORPUS*. The regions are large; it is difficult to make them smaller and to keep the size of the Board financially and organizationally manageable.

Regional coordinators are, for many, the most visible sign that *CORPUS* seeks close contact with its members. Regional activity enables information to reach the membership and to get to the Board; regional meetings bring speakers, social interaction, liturgical celebration, and support, within the limits that geography and energy permit.

CORPUS has invested considerable resources into the member services office, assuring that everyone's communication (our toll-free number is 888-2-PRIEST), from around the nation and the world, is answered or referred to the appropriate committee or expert in the field.

Without the regions and member services, *CORPUS* would be less a community than it is.

▷ *Transition*

We have been diligent as a presence and support, sometimes with emergency financial assistance (through the Warren Barker Foundation and members' donations), sometimes as a canonical advocate for married priests and their families. Through attorney Paul McGreevy we have supported a national effort to secure married priests pension rights. Most of all we help married priests to sense their dignity and their calling and we send them forth with a pastoral mandate to serve God's People.

THE SPIRIT OF *CORPUS*

This section of our report will be of greater interest. Many of us may have been more aware of the structural changes. It is useful, nonetheless, to survey them so that we are accountable to the membership, so that people may realize that our movement has been not only intentional but very concrete, and so that we can see the means *CORPUS* takes to renew the spirit of married priests.

Many in *CORPUS* see our purpose as the canonical reintegration of married priests. And so it is. The mistake may be in measuring the success of this movement by that standard alone. Canonical reintegration will come about but it may receive a mixed reaction from CORPUS members, especially if the church at large remains substantially unreformed.

Canonical reintegration depends less on us than a renewal of spirit does. This is the true measure, I believe, of the worth of CORPUS. It is not our canonical standing but what has happened to our hearts which matters.

It is my intention to cite the themes CORPUS pursued in the renewal of the lives of its members. The themes are not assigned priorities. We must do this on our own, in our individual dialogues with ourselves and with God.

▷ Solidarity

One of the most painful experiences in resigning is a sense of isolation. Until CORPUS came on the scene, many married priests believed they were few in number; they found communication with other married priests difficult; they felt vulnerable and misunderstood.

CORPUS created a community where the married priesthood could be not only accepted but, much more, celebrated. The powerful experiences of ordination, transition, and marriage enabled us to share a common meaning and ministry. This gave us a unique mission and, indeed, a sense of joy and permanent happiness as we discovered one another and became colleagues in a new life.

▷ Vocation

The married priesthood is a calling.

There are those in the church who do not believe that God calls us and gives us the gift of a new vocation. They link this new life of ours with shame or guilt, branding our marriages as broken promises, our choices as self indulgent, our life of love as sinful or inferior. But we know, in the core of our souls, that our marriages were a work of grace and that this calling possesses the same sacred integrity that ordination did.

The women we married and the children we nurtured gave us the priesthood in a new form.

▷ *Witness*

CORPUS is not essentially a political force in the church. It is a testimony, a witness, a sacrament of what God has done with us and for us. It is a manifestation of the power of relationship in the formation of pastoral ministers. It is a proclamation that women are sources of grace in the lives of priests and that sexual love is sacred. Indeed, we have learned that faithfulness is rooted in the commitments we make to people and the community we share with them.

We do not bear witness to the fact that marriage is easy or that married priests are without flaws. But we do learn in marriage how concrete and inescapable forgiveness is and how impossible it is to live without the endorsement of those we love.

▷ *Education*

CORPUS has been an educational resource for married priests and for the church at large. It has redefined our sense of theology and church law. It has formulated different rules for belonging to the church and it has shown that these rules are sound by the faithful love they create for the church and for its people.

There was so much church history we did not know; so much of the church's life we did not see; so many alternatives which were unknown to us. Jesus once told us that we can judge life by the fruit it bears. Our educational efforts have borne the fruit of love in our families and in the compassion we feel for marginalized people in our church and in the world.

▷ *Reform*

CORPUS is not primarily a political force but it does seek change, in attitude and structure, in our church. All true prophecy has political implications.

We have been led by our life in *CORPUS* to reformulate the essence of priesthood as inclusive rather than clerical, as somehow dependent on us and not only on the definitions or limits the institutional church draws. We want to share this with all God's People, with the pope and bishops, with celibate priests and women religious and all the baptized. We seek to share this because we have found an abundance of life and happiness and we cannot keep this to ourselves.

▷ *Collaboration*

CORPUS helped us to sense the breadth and character of the world-wide movement for reform. It made us participants and collaborators with those who sought justice for women and the recognition of rights in the church.

The world-wide reform movement has about it the resonance of a new reformation or pentecost, endorsed not only by Vatican II but also by the gospel. The resonance has not always been perceived by church administrators but it has been heard by reformers and committed Catholics in this nation and around the world. *CORPUS* has magnified the sound of this movement and called us to a symphony of collaboration, creativity, and harmony with men and women around the world. In the presence of *CORPUS*, cardinals, bishops and canonical priests have told us that they too are reformers and that they pray for our work and wish us success.

Sometimes we find colleagues in *COR*, sometimes in the International Federation of Married Catholic Priests, sometimes in "We Are Church." It matters not what name they bear. If they see the signs of the times and yearn for a new church as Vatican II once saw it, they are ours, our brothers and sisters, and we are theirs.

242

▷ *Freedom*

I can attest to the fact that I have felt enormous freedom in my own life because of my decision to marry and to belong to the church as a married priest. I have seen the exuberance of freedom in the lives of countless *CORPUS* members. Each one must answer for himself or herself about whether this is true or not.

The freedom, as I have known it, is not a freedom to do as one chooses as though nothing mattered except one's own agenda or life. It has been a freedom of remarkable creativity and of profound fidelity to all that existed in the promise of my ordination and to all that is present in my affirmation of myself as a Catholic. It is, if I may be bold enough to say this, a freedom of the Spirit, so bracing in its power that it takes me time and again down roads I did not initially choose. I keep finding God on these roads, some of them Damascus-like, others similar to the road from Jericho to Jerusalem where one finds people battered by life, still others like the roads that brought a prodigal son home. The great miracle of Jesus was the freedom he gave by liberating people from disease or discrimination, from a sense of worthlessness or a feeling God did not care for them. It is such freedom I feel now and *CORPUS* has helped me not to be frightened by freedom of such magnitude and, indeed, to help bring this about in others.

▷ *Poverty*

It is foolish to pretend there have not been losses. There is no need for such pretension, not if one finds meaning and love.

For most, the transition process was a death-like experience. For many, there was poverty in financial terms, sometimes desperate in its destitution. For others, there has been the loss of a spouse, the death of a child, losses they would not have endured as celibate priests. For some, there was estrangement of parents or siblings or the withering of spirit that goes with employment one did not prefer or the heart-ache of feeling the injustice of exclusion from a ministry they loved and did so well.

243

CORPUS has allowed the grief to be named and shared. It has permitted the sorrow expression, not in self-pity, but for the sake of truth and healing. The price of pain was a worthy exchange for the priceless treasure of marriage and children and a non-clerical ministry.

CORPUS has been an assembly of the poor and the disenfranchised as well as a community of the redeemed and renewed. Many *CORPUS* priests encountered poverty as they had never known it in canonical service. The poverty led some to bitterness but many more found a need for God and love on levels they did not think possible.

▷ *A Discipleship of Equals*

The *CORPUS* agenda has won the minds and hearts of Catholics. A married priesthood is their preference, worldwide, by substantial margins.

Lay members of *CORPUS* sit on our Board and hold elective office, organize our annual conferences and write regularly in our publications.

Marriage and children are special, shared experiences with laity. Most of all, non-clerical ministry makes us part of a discipleship of equals. No one of us serves by ecclesiastical mandate. All of us are called forth by the need people have for us and by their choice to make us ministers of word and sacrament in their lives. We do not come with titles or canonical privileges, with distinctive dress and institutional authority. We are, as we have never been before, servants of the gospel and people.

In all of this we feel a distinct kinship with our brothers and sisters in Protestant churches. We are often welcome there and we find in such churches that our wives are honored and our ministries endorsed. If this helps Christian unity advance, then all of us win and the gospel prevails.

▷ *Spirituality*

If we lost God or Christ along the way, then we are indeed lost. St. Paul said it well when he observed that for him to win is Christ.

We in *CORPUS* have noticed that many people whom no canonical priest would reach have been brought into a sense of God and Christ and church by our ministry. They in turn have taught us a great deal about priesthood and compassion, about human decency and love both within and beyond the canonical rules.

It has been a spiritual journey. We found God in places where we were told God could not be found. And we rejoiced because we came to understand anew that God is everywhere and that love is always possible. We rejoiced because we found salvation is as universal as human need and that the priesthood can take on as many forms as life allows. We have seen that there are many ways to be Catholic and that these new ways are not at odds with the substantial tradition of the church and the gospel message. We might not have seen this or we might deny having seen this had we remained in canonical service.

We always knew God existed beyond the boundaries of the institutional church but we did not know as well as we do now that God exists with equal intensity everywhere and that there are no special places for God to dwell. Jesus tried to teach us this when he proclaimed God's Presence beyond the Temple and the Sabbath, beyond the Jewish priesthood and even its religion. We understand this message better now.

It has been a blessed journey. We must admit this. Even the anguish. Certainly the joy.

We found God here, in our lives, with our spouses, surrounded by our children, in the midst of those who needed us. We found God in our choices, in our relationships and in our calling. *CORPUS* helped us celebrate this and, in doing so, redeemed its promise.

REDEEMING HUMANITY
Redemption and Integrity

L ate, in the second century, a seventeen–year old man wrote to his father, Leonides, who was awaiting martyrdom. The letter urged him to go to his death bravely, with no anxiety for his family of seven children.

The young man himself yearned to die as a martyr. His mother barely kept him steady and hid his clothes to prevent him from begging the Romans to kill him. The young man was brilliant but volatile and erratic.

He defined himself as the "son of a martyr", a title he treasured. He grew despondent, however, as the opportunity for martyrdom receded and as his sexual temptations intensified.

Three years after his father's execution, the young man, now twenty, found a physician and asked to be castrated. In the blood of that mutilation, the young man believed his humanity was redeemed.

We are speaking of Origen, sometimes cited, with good reason, as one of the most brilliant thinkers who ever lived. But Origen is a troubled man living in a troubled century.

ORIGEN

To evaluate the Origen story, we might raise a few questions. Why, for example, was the celibacy of Jesus so different from that of

247

Origen? Why can we not imagine Jesus acting as Origen did or expecting his disciples to do such violence?

The difference lies in the fact that Jesus saw his celibacy as an item of lesser significance and Origen considered celibacy the defining event of his life. Jesus was not primarily a celibate; he was a prophet whose celibacy made sense only in the context of prophecy and of his own personal life. Jesus makes no reference to his celibacy, and he does not make it a condition of discipleship. A prophet or an apostle for that matter might just as well have been married, in the thinking of Jesus, as Isaiah was or as Peter is. The New Testament church makes so little of the celibacy of Jesus that when Paul speaks of the excellence of celibacy, he makes no reference to the celibacy of Jesus. Jesus is a prophet, not *the* celibate. When Paul forcefully proclaims his celibacy to the Corinthians, he refrains from asking the Corinthian church as a whole to follow his example. It is almost a century after Jesus before any of his disciples base their celibacy on his example.

By the time we get to Origen, celibacy becomes more important than prophecy; indeed, celibacy is seen by many as the prophetic witness.

There is more to this issue. The difference between Jesus and Origen lies in their attitude toward the Spirit. Jesus believed the Spirit came to everyone and might lead a disciple in any marital direction. The quality of the heart was the substantive work of the Spirit, not conjugal or celibate choices. For Origen, the Spirit prefers celibates. A hierarchical order gains ground in the Christian community, based on authority and the renunciation of sexual experience. In the course of subsequent church history, the alliance between authority and celibacy will continue.

The castration of Origen derives from an unhealthy admixture of arrogance and despair. The arrogance is the assumption that he could control the Holy Spirit by destroying his body and that he could become thereby a part of an elite celibate corps of distinguished Christians. The despair is in the supposition that the Holy Spirit does not love us unless we renounce ourselves and mutilate ourselves physically or emotionally. Origen's castration generates a sad and savage spirituality and, in the next generation, a church of force and power.

Origen's celibacy is based on two themes the New Testament church would have found bizarre. In the first instance, he uses his celibacy as a power base to support prophetic or apostolic leadership in the church. Until Origen, pastoral care of the church was given by married heads of households who function as the priests and bishops of the first two centuries. From Origen forward, the church will be governed by celibates, by and large, by men without family life, living a lifestyle deemed superior and more spiritual. Origen's castration eventually cuts off married pastors from the life of the community.

A second theme in Origen changes the tradition. Origen teaches the supremacy of life–long virginity. Until Origen, celibacy was a choice people might make after the death of a spouse rather than for their whole life. In this context, celibacy and marriage complemented each other and both might serve the pastoral office or the spiritual life equally well.

Why did Origen's thinking have such an impact? It was due, I believe, to an unusual convergence of culture and politics in the next two centuries. The culture of Greek asceticism became the fashionable way to redeem or develop one's humanity. This asceticism preferred martyrdom to life, the desert to the community, virginity to family, men to women. Within a century of Origin's death, Ambrose declares that all that is best in the teaching of Jesus is in Plato. Celibacy, he continues, is the one experience which distinguishes us from the beasts of the field. The writers of the New Testament would have been startled at such assertions.

It is time for another story.

AUGUSTINE

The woman had been with him since he was eighteen. Even then, she knew he was brilliant. Everyone knew that. A year after they began to live together, she had a son. Now, after thirteen years, he told her she must go away, at a time when he and their son especially needed her. He chose never to write or even, for all we know, to speak her name after her departure, as though the refusal to name her would make it seem she never existed or made a difference.

He loved her, in his own way, more perhaps than he ever loved anyone else. The wound of her leaving never fully healed. It bled in different ways throughout his life, as guilt and loss, as anger and longing, as envy and insecurity. She was always there somehow, competing with God for his attention although neither she nor God saw themselves as competitors. The last words she spoke to him were a vow, that she would never love or live with any other man for the rest of her life. Five year after she left, the boy, whom the father kept, died at the age of seventeen.

The man, of course, is Augustine; the boy is Adeodatus; the woman is anonymous. We are in the fourth century.

Augustine dismissed his companion driven not by a law of celibacy but by a psychological need to excel and become perfect. If you were Augustine, you would understand. His age found the body loathsome. He had been a Manichean for nine years and learned that the body was "blood and bile and flatulence and excrement...a mold of defilement." Ambrose, his mentor, and he himself saw sex as a body function and could not link it with love or grace or relationship. Augustine, with his insatiable sexual appetites, saw the mother of his son as a co–conspirator in lust. He cut off his sexual life with her as sharply as Origen had once done his own.

Augustine won a mighty victory over himself but there were victims. The institutional church and clerical celibacy gain a mighty champion but a nameless woman and, perhaps, Adeodatus and even Augustine himself and indeed, the future church may all have been wounded by the ordeal and the achievement. It is a question worth raising, is it not?

Augustine speaks of Adeodatus from time to time as the years accumulate. Some months before Adeodatus dies, he expresses his pride in the boy's intelligence; in the last book he writes, he speaks of his son as someone a father is happy to have surpassed him "in all things." But there is always the ambivalence. He conceived

Adeodatus in wickedness. Even had he been married, that would not have helped. Augustine believed sex was always wrong. " I had no part in that boy," he writes, "except the sin." Fortunately, Adeodatus had died before Augustine wrote that sentence.

We must not become sentimental or naive. Augustine, as a married man, might have developed less effectively. Celibacy, after all, for many is a creative way to live. Saints such as Francis of Assisi, mystics such as Teresa of Avila are remarkably impressive people.

The sadness of Augustine lies in the fact that the church had encouraged a climate of necessity about celibacy and Augustine became a driven man. The problem is not celibacy but the fact that Augustine saw no meaningful alternative to it.

By the end of the fourth century, as a result of Origen and Augustine, respect for marriage has vanished; much of the value Jesus gave women in his preaching is gone.

"How sordid, filthy and horrible a woman's embraces," Augustine writes of wives. Hear the anger in the words. Yet Augustine is honest enough to express the ambivalence. During the day, he tells us, he is sure sex is evil but at night, as he reviews what he has preached, he wonders if he is right and if things are so one–sided.

A final vignette of Augustine. Near the end of his life, he conducts a bitter debate with Julian, a bishop who espouses Pelagianism. Pelagianism asserts that people are basically good even without baptism. Augustine vigorously disagrees. Seldom in church history do we behold a great and brilliant man so much at the mercy of his blind spots. Julian was the son of a bishop and married the daughter of a bishop. Allow me to summarize the debate.

Julian: If you are right, Augustine, that original sin is in our very nature, it seems the devil is as much a maker of human beings as God. Do I hear in this the Manicheanism you once accepted? When you declare without equivocation that all new born children are evil until baptized, I shudder. When you add that you have found the source of evil and it is in our genitals, I am disgusted, affronted by this insult to God, our Creator.

Augustine: All human beings, infants included, are lost without baptism. God does not redeem humanity, only the elect. The proof that evil is in our genitals is our shame and, especially, those sexual feelings which stir us against our better judgment, reflecting the disobedience of a higher law which Adam initiated.

Julian: Sexual feeling is not evil. It is a sense in our body, like seeing or hearing, put there by God to make us aware of who we are.

Augustine: If people listen to you, Julian, they will "jump, into bed whenever they like...tickled by desire unable to wait until dark." Is this what you want for God's people? I hear not the voice of truth but the sort of sexual life you and your wife lead. Keep your sexual experience out of this debate.

Julian: We're not arguing about sex but about God. Your God punishes infants in eternal fire. Where is your compassion, your common sense? A God who tortures infants commits a crime disgusting to barbarians, let alone Christians.

Augustine: If unbaptized infants are saved, God is not sovereign. If human nature is good, why did Christ redeem us? If salvation is easy, what is the worth of our sacrifices, the women we send away, the children we do not generate, the sexual pleasure we reject?

Augustine's view prevails with Rome and the papacy. The anger and irrationality of Augustine in this debate are disturbing. Is it because Julian was the son of a bishop and was himself about the same age as Adeodatus would have been had he lived? Was the real adversary not Julian but Augustine himself? Was the anger directed not at false teaching but at forced celibacy?

By the end of the fourth century, celibacy is the prestigious and spiritually superior life choice for a priest.

WHO BROUGHT THIS TO PASS?

Primarily, Origen and Augustine, even though there were many others. Origen and Augustine show how successful men of social position and elite education can live in cities and become spiritually exalted through celibacy, and substantial personal sacrifices.

252

Both men are also talented publicists of their own lives and theories.

WHY DID THIS OCCUR?

A cast of characters, including hermits and desert ascetics, bishops such as John Chrysostom and scholars such as Jerome, bring the Greek fear of the body, sex and women into the church and give it respectability and status. Christianity's powerful influence in the Roman Empire allow it the resources and legal potential to institutionalize celibacy as the preferred alternative for a cleric. Since Christianity controls Western and Eastern Europe, celibacy brings enormous career and economic advantages. Even marriage is considered holy only insofar as it approximates the celibate ideal. The best marriages for all Christians are those which are sexless; in the marriages of clerics, this sexlessness becomes obligatory. The famous Council of Elvira, meeting in Spain in 305, decrees that all clerics are "ordered to abstain completely from their wives and not to have children." This Council does not deal with clerical celibacy, as many suppose, but with celibate clerical marriages.

WHY DOES THIS HAPPEN?

The process takes two centuries and is complete by the fourth century. The married head of household leadership in the church of the first centuries vanishes.

I do not suggest that some of the choices for celibacy during this period are not motivated by idealism and love. Nor that choices for marriage were always noble. I do suggest that the behavior and belief of the institutional church in enforcing celibacy and defaming marriage were appalling.

"I have found where evil lives," Augustine cries out as the fourth century ends. "It lives in the genitals. See the place. *Ecce unde. Ecce unde.* See where the evil lives, in your body, in your sex organs, in your pleasure."

Is it naive to ask :Where is Jesus Christ in all this? Where is the splendor of marriage and the miracle of children? Why had the glory of God's creation been dishonored and shamed?

THE TWELFTH CENTURY

We move forward now six centuries.

The psychological pressure to choose celibacy is enormous during the intervening centuries. The married priesthood continues, however, even though priests and their wives often are defamed, sometimes forcibly separated, always under suspicion.

There are, nonetheless, married popes late into the ninth century (Adrian II, who dies in 872, is married). Even after Lateran II in 1139 and the prohibition of marriage to all priests, there are married bishops throughout Europe. The major dioceses of England persist in choosing married bishops; Ely, London, Salisbury, Durham, Winchester. Law is viewed very differently in the twelfth century. Papal and conciliar prohibitions are considered position papers rather than legal regulations as we now understand them.

The contention that church tradition never sanctioned marriage after ordination for priests is simply not true.

Bishop Rather of Verona, Italy, observes in the tenth century, that priests arranged marriages for their daughters to other priests and that if he expelled all priests who live with women or who marry after ordination, there would be no one left (PL 136, 491). Bishop Otto of Constance, Germany, gives permission for unmarried priests to marry (cf. Ranke–Heinemann). In 1076, Archbishop Lanfranc of Canterbury, England, forbids clerics to marry after ordination (implying that the practice was widespread) but allows all priests already married to keep their wives, without distinguishing whether they married before or after ordination (cf. Barstow). The situation is fluid and bishops, in great numbers, apparently accept marriage after ordination. Rome, at this point, does not have the resources or, perhaps, the will to stop the practice. At a time when all marriage is considered a spiritual compromise, we cannot expect church leaders to propose marriage after ordination. More telling is the fact that married men continue to be ordained in commanding numbers even though marriage is judged negatively. How much more fitting today is a married priesthood, when

254

marriage is honored!

Let us move now to Ravenna, Italy. The year is 1007 and a baby, born to an impoverished mother of a large family, is starving to death. The mother ignores the cries because the family does not have the means to raise him. A neighboring woman, ironically the wife of a married priest, saves the infant's life by begging the mother to nurse him. The child grows up to become a vicious adversary of married priests and their wives. This is Peter Damian. A century after he begins to preach, Second Lateran will terminate the married priesthood and the church will order the break up of married priests' families.

A few portraits may give us insights into the climate of the late eleventh and early twelfth centuries as church leaders tear our a tradition of married priesthood with roots in the New Testament.

In this final century of optional celibacy, Peter Damian brings to bear the psychological warfare begun by Origen and developed by Augustine. His intent is different from theirs; he seeks a law, a conciliar decree and papal support to end priests' marriages. Since all other measures have failed, force will be used.

Damian presents a classic argument on sex and ritual purity. He warns priests and their wives or whores as he calls them: "The hands that touch the body and blood of Christ must not touch the genitals of a whore." In a pitch of hysteria, he sees women as "flesh of the devil," "cause of our ruin," "the very stuff of sin," "pigs". Even Peter the Apostle does not escape censure: "Peter washed away the filth of his marriage with the blood of his martyrdom." Peter Damian, I might add, is a canonized saint of the Catholic church.

In 1105, a young man, Serio of Bayeux, France, the son of a priest, is discharged from his benefice or inheritance because of a recent ruling of pope Urban II. Priests' sons are forbidden the right to be ordained. The law seeks to deprive them of any inheritance they might have received from their fathers.

Serio defends himself with some startling observations.

The new law, he argues, denies the equality of all Christians conferred by baptism. Ordination and law are utilized to make

Christians unequal. To deny ordination to a man only because he is the son of a priest is punitive rather than pastoral, economic in its intent rather than evangelical.

He goes on to observe that the popes of the eleventh and twelfth century are obsessively committed to controlling the church. Serio's point is well taken. Gregory VII, one of the most absolutist popes in church history, declared a few decades before this, in 1075, that a pope can depose all princes since the pope alone rules both the temporal and the religious world. The unyielding character of Gregory VII dismayed friends who found his sometimes single–minded fanaticism occasionally idealistic but often terrifying. church history shows that the more autocratic the pope, the more rigid he is on obligatory celibacy.

The third point made by Serio is the most delicate. He charges that homosexual clergy are dominant and that they influence the movement to terminate the married priesthood.

Serio's comment appears accurate. John Boswell, professor of history at Yale, documents the record in his landmark book, *Christianity, Social Tolerance, and Homosexuality.* He demonstrates that the century from 1050–1150, the century of Peter Damian, Gregory VII, and Second Lateran is a century in which homosexuality flourished in he clergy. Numerous commentators of the day complain about monasteries as homosexual centers; they raise questions about why severe laws are passed forbidding heterosexual relations in clerical marriages while no regulations are promulgated prohibiting homosexual relations in monasteries.

If the preponderance of homosexuals is true, the motive driving the Second Lateran becomes all the more suspect. Monks had achieved great power and controlled the legislative centers of the church at this time. Gregory VII was a monk and at least six other popes of the period. In citing this data, I do not wish to imply any judgmental attitude toward homosexuality.

As the twelfth century ends, a different church emerges. It is a church exclusively centered in the Western and Latin Rite, a church in which the pope is supreme not only as bishop but as ruler of Europe. Canon Law assumes enormous importance and obligatory celibacy is a universal requirement for priests.

I suggest that obligatory celibacy requires a context similar to that of the twelfth century to prevail. The papacy must be seen as absolute and human sexuality must be considered an evil. church law must become normative for Christian behavior and the world must be judged deficient and decadent. Since these conditions no longer exist or are even possible, obligatory celibacy cannot endure.

The more democratic a culture, the more imperative it is for church leaders to explain obligations in ways people at large and priests in particular can understand and approve.

Obligatory celibacy is not beyond the capabilities of clergy and Catholics today; it is simply beyond their preferences. It is not preferred because it functions best in a medieval rather than in a modern world. Celibacy as an option is praiseworthy; as an obligation, it is an anachronism.

As Julian observed in his debate with Augustine, when marriage and women and sexuality are devalued, we are not arguing about the marital condition of a priest. We are raising questions about what we think of God and the church and how we perceive family life and human freedom.

We are speaking about redeeming humanity and what it is in us which needs redemption. We do not need to be redeemed from the world or from marriage, from women or from sexual experience, from freedom or from the signs of the times. Not a single one of these items is evil. All were made by God. We need only be redeemed from our misuse of these values and, especially, from the arrogance of imposing our will on others.

REDEEMING THE CHURCH FOR HUMANITY

We now know the main actors in the elimination of the married priesthood.

WHO ARE THEY?

Origen and Augustine and Damian were major protagonists. Who today would want to defend obligatory celibacy with the arguments they used to enforce it?There were others, of course. Over so long a period of time, there had to be. Jerome and Crysostom, synods, and councils, homosexual clerics and sexually frightened heterosexuals, reforming popes and ambitious bishops, some saints and a few mystics, all played a part. The canvas is too vast to limit the scene to only the few we have named.

To Origen, Augustine and Damian, I would add two other major influences: Gregory VII and the Second Lateran Council

A footnote might be in order. Many know that Second Lateran terminated the married priesthood in 1139. We are often less informed on the pope who called that Council. His name was Innocent II and his election was so notorious that it began an eight year schism. His predecessor died on February 13, 1130 and was hastily buried. In the middle of that night, a minority of cardinals elected him and staged an illegal coronation ceremony at daybreak of February 14. People met the new pope before knowing the former pope was dead and buried. A majority of cardinals called the election invalid and chose another pope. Innocent II's claims were reinforced by armies from England, Germany and France. The schism ended with the death of the contender in 1138. Innocent and that Council terminate the married priesthood.

WHY DID THIS HAPPEN?

The married priesthood ended because of intense zeal for sexless lives by men who denigrated marriage, sexual experience and women. There were also questions of power and property. Nor must we omit a defective sacramental theology which saw the Eucharist violated by marital sexual love. Some were well intentioned and believed, no doubt, that God and Christ wished this, but even these despaired of human nature and the Holy Spirit and found violence acceptable. The preaching of Jesus about respect and love for one another and his efforts to persuade his disciples to choose values from internal conviction were scuttled so that the Kingdom of God might become the institutional church.

WHEN DID THIS HAPPEN?

It happened in two stages. The second to the fourth centuries psychologically destroyed the respect for marriage, sex, and women. The eleventh and twelfth centuries banned the married priesthood by law and moved to create an imperial church.

The past is best interpreted by its consequences. We did not know well what the voyages of Columbus meant until North and South America created the nations and cultures which came after him. We see Magna Carta in a different light after the American Constitution and the French Revolution.

Whatever the reasons for obligatory celibacy in the past, its consequences are hurting the church now, wounding it grievously. The world at large and the church as the whole body of Christ have opted for a reformed and renewed priesthood, a liberated and honest church, a ministry and community vastly different from that proposed by reactionary forces in Rome.

The issue, however, is much more than obligatory celibacy. The issue is God and the church as a community. It is humanity and people as a family, It is women and their dignity as persons. We are really dealing with freedom and the gospel, the celebration of creation and gratitude for our bodies. The subject is not sex. On its deepest levels, it has something to do with faith and how we are redeemed and whether that redemption is joyful and sensitive to our most profound needs as human beings and the essential integrity of our lives.

SUGGESTED READINGS

Married Priests and the Reforming Papacy;
The Eleventh–Century Debates.
Ann Llewellyn Barstow.
(Edwin Mellen Press, New York,, 1982).

Augustine of Hippo: A Biography.
Peter Brown (University of California Press, 1967)

The Boday and Society, Men, Women and
Sexual Renunciation in Early Christianity.
Peter Brown (Columbia University Press, 1990)

Sexual Practices and the Medieval church.
Vern L. Bullough and James Brundage.
(Prometheus Books, Buffalo, 1982).

Eunuchs for the Kingdom of Heaven.
Ute Ranke–Heinemann (Doubleday, 1990)

REDEEMING HUMANITY

A HOMILY:
DO YOU LOVE ME?
The Last Dialogue Between Christ and Peter

"Do you love me?....Feed my sheep...when you grow old,
you will stretch out your hands....
Follow Me."

JOHN 21: 15-19

These were probably the last words between them. Jesus and Peter. Two strong personalities, speaking about endings. Jesus, about to depart. Peter, adjusting to absence and learning about his death.

The words are charged, heavily charged, with powerful feelings.

Jesus speaks about the love they shared together and he asks Peter to take care of all that Jesus loved and was leaving.

I wonder if Peter recalled those words forty years later, on the night before he died, at his own last supper. He remembered them, surely, the next morning, on the cross, dying as Jesus himself had died.

The final words of Jesus and Peter sum up ministry and priesthood, discipleship and the gospel.

Jesus speaks of love. Love is always first in the mind and heart of Jesus.

263

Peter, do you love me? The primary relationship between Jesus and Peter is not law or order or obedience or deference. It is love.

Men do not speak easily of love but they do so readily when they face death together. On battlefields, before execution, in beds as they lay dying.

Men weep easily in trenches and jungles, proclaiming their love and loyalty for one another, their friendship, their awful loss as death pursues them. Jesus and Peter speak of death and departure in this passage and so words of love are not unfitting. By speaking in advance of Peter's death, Jesus promises to be there in some deep, mysterious, and faithful way. The Risen Christ is present in all our dying. Peter, however, was absent when Jesus died. He never forgot that. Even at the end.

Did Peter think of love on the cross the morning he died? How could he not have?

These final words of love between Jesus and Peter define the office and ministry Jesus left the church.

I like to think that Peter remembered his wife too as he died. She was part of all this, for many years. Men generally marry women whose hearts are moved by similar values.

We do not know her name but Paul tells us that she went on missionary journeys with Peter.

It is not surprising. Love does such things.

Women who love go with men on all the impossible roads they take. They bring love into what men would make only a mission.

Peter must have wept on the cross, the way the gospels tell us he did when he thought he lost Christ because of his denial and desertion. How could he not think of this as he stretched out his hands in death? The comfort would have come in the memory of that final dialogue. "Do you love me? Follow me."

Do we want to know what priesthood is? It is this. Learning to love so strongly that it breaks your heart and makes your soul weep. Regretting that you did not love enough. Rejoicing when you did. Peter loved that way.

It is never enough to love God. Jesus told us this. We must love one another as well. We are expected to give our lives for one another. This is priesthood also.

How could Peter not feel such love for the wife who shared his journey? How could he die without her name also in his heart?

We are moved in this liturgy by a Christ who asks if we still have love, for him, for the community of disciples we call the church, for everyone.

Peter is not a young man at the end. But he loves Christ with a young love, for all that Christ gave him (ministry, mission, marriage) and for all that Christ asked (love, fidelity, sacrifice).

A further issue Jesus and Peter talk about in their last conversation is taking care of all Jesus left behind and could not stop loving. "Feed my sheep." Note, they are not Peter's sheep.

Christ says, in effect, Do not feed them, Peter, with stones when they need bread, with law when they need life, with the hierarchical priesthood when they need a companion, with your safety when they need your wounds, with your certitudes when they need your doubts, with you indifference when they need your passion.

Nothing nourishes us except love. To feed and tend the flock of God's People, only love will do.

Peter's life did not go as he envisioned or intended. He was expelled from the original Jewish community he was deeply committed to as a young man. He led the Christian community in ways he did not anticipate and did not always prefer.

But if you love, this is what you do. You do not hold on to what you once were—not if you are in love, you don't. And so Peter didn't.

When Peter first met Jesus on the shores of Galilee he never envisioned that they would meet years later on a cross. The journey, it seems, creates its own meaning, beyond our designs.

Peter did not have to be a priest, or even Kephas. He had to be who he was meant to be.

So much irony in the new name, Peter. Peter is a rock. The gospel tells us he was hardly that. He wept readily. He was often confused. Jesus at times was exasperated with him. And, of course, he ran away when Jesus needed him most. Once he almost drowned. There is something a little comical in that. He must have felt stupid when he returned to the boat. Hardly a rock. Except that he sank like one.

Peter was often terrified. He went down roads he had not expected and lost enormously along the way. Life and love demand that we don't try to keep all as it was.

Peter's fallibility endears him to the Christian community. Christians love Peter more easily than Paul, in large measure, because of the courage which comes through the weakness. We admire Paul but we love Peter.

What was Peter at the end?

A Pilgrim of Conscience—someone who had to hear Christ and the Spirit in his heart and conscience because there were no structures or rules or maps to guide him where he had to go. It was a new journey taken for his own sake and for the sake of God's People. This was the only way he could be Peter rather than the Kephas he once was.

What was he at the end?

The elder brother of a people of hope. He became a source of strength because he was always defined not by what he decided he could do for the People of Hope but by what they needed from him.

He did not see himself as infallible. The gospels show him acting collegially, with the Twelve and with the community, able to

266

listen as Paul rebukes him, apparently without defending himself.

Peter wanted only to heal and to be healed, to feed and to be fed by the Word of God.

On the cross, he is left with his memories and his love—memories of his wife, of the people he cured, of the God for whose sake he was ready to die, of that first Easter morning and of the last dialogue with Christ.

He must have died with words of forgiveness. Jesus taught him that. Jesus died like that. I hope the forgiveness included Peter's forgiveness of himself.

Had Peter held onto everything he once was he would have died as Kephas, somewhere in Galilee, a fisherman. Because he gave up so much out of love he lives on as Peter, still able to touch our hearts in the simplicity and sincerity of his love. What he became at the end was due not only to Christ but to the nameless wife he loved through all the changing names and missions and seasons of his life.

You only validate people when you are willing to sacrifice for them, even give your life for them. That's what priesthood is all about, what it was meant to be, an imitation, a following, of a Christ who did that for us. That's what the church is for—validation and love, and losses, catastrophic losses, of life and ministry if need be, losses which strangely are not losses if you let them go for the sake of love.